4

NATURAL THEOLOGY

The Library of Liberal Arts
OSKAR PIEST, FOUNDER

The Library of Liberal Arts

NATURAL THEOLOGY

Selections

WILLIAM PALEY

Edited, with an introduction, by

FREDERICK FERRÉ

Associate Professor of Philosophy, Dickinson College

The Library of Liberal Arts

published by

 THE **BOBBS-MERRILL** COMPANY, INC.
A SUBSIDIARY OF HOWARD W. SAMS & CO., INC.
Publishers • INDIANAPOLIS • NEW YORK

William Paley: 1743-1805

NATURAL THEOLOGY was originally published in 1802

. . . .

CONTENTS
· · · · · · · · · · · · · · · · ·

NATURAL THEOLOGY: SELECTIONS¹

¹ Following is a Table of Contents for the complete work; material
omitted in this edition has been bracketed.

INTRODUCTION

I

William Paley began his life at Peterborough, England, in 1743—just four years after Hume's *Treatise of Human Nature* had fallen "dead-born from the press" and Wesley's first lay preachers, hearts "strangely warmed," had ignited the Methodist revival in fields near Bristol. Today Paley is primarily remembered for the path he tried to illuminate between the skeptical intellectualism of the one and the pious enthusiasm of the other. His culminating work, *Natural Theology* (1802), can perhaps best be interpreted as an attempt to show that theistic belief rests on a more secure foundation than Wesley's emotionalism and that reason is capable of leading beyond Hume's doubt and negativity.

Historically, of course, one must acknowledge that Paley was explicitly concerned with neither of these giants of his century. Amazing as it may appear, our author does not even refer to Hume by name in a period when, it may seem to us today, the only important task for philosophical thinkers was to wrestle with the challenging Scotsman. But the situation was not so obvious at the time. James Beattie (1735-1803), in his *Essay on Truth* (1770), was supposed by all "right-minded" persons from Dr. Johnson to George III (who kept a copy of the *Essay* at both his primary residences) to have refuted Hume. And Kant, despite the efforts of young Coleridge to interpret Germany to Britain, was not yet widely known. Such considerations help to explain the strange fact that Paley's *Natural Theology* seems to fall out of chronological order: in it the superlative statement of the teleological argument was reached, but only after Hume and Kant had inflicted on that argument their heavy blows.

It was not for being supposed philosophically out-of-date, then, that Paley's rise in the Church of England was less high than his considerable talents might have warranted. On the contrary, the primary obstacles to his career were his liberal and forward-looking political views in a society fearful of revolutions. Largely on this account Paley's advancement in the Church failed to fulfill his early promise at Giggleswick School, where his father was headmaster, and at Christ's College, Cambridge, where he pursued his studies with great distinction. After his graduation from Cambridge in 1763, Paley soon gained the honor of becoming a fellow there in 1766 and a tutor in 1768, the year after his ordination. His success as a lecturer was brilliant, as might be guessed from the lucidity of his written style. Among other liberal causes (such as the abolition of slavery) Paley supported the campaign of his benefactor, Bishop Law, for the reformation and simplification of the Thirty-nine Articles. Eventually he married, in 1776, giving up his fellowship at Cambridge and retiring to a small "living" in Westmoreland. Receiving a variety of ecclesiastical appointments, he reached his highest post, archdeacon of Carlisle, England, in 1782.

It was only after this time that Paley's energies were turned toward writing. His first book, comprising the substance of his lectures on moral philosophy (in which field he, with Bentham, was one of the founders of the Utilitarian school), was published as *The Principles of Moral and Political Philosophy* in 1785 and became an immediate success. Adopted as a standard textbook at Cambridge, the *Principles* went through nearly a score of editions in Paley's own lifetime. Five years later *Horae Paulinae* appeared, followed in 1794 by a second book in Christian apologetics, his *View of the Evidences of Christianity*. Finally, three years before his death in 1805, Paley published his best-known—if not most original—work, *Natural Theology, or Evidences of the Existence and Attributes of the Deity collected from the Appearances of Nature*.

The fact that *Natural Theology* was not to any large extent original has never diminished its importance. Paley, in this book, acts as an expositor, not as an originator. His great service was to express more lucidly than anyone before him the theological theory which underlay, though vaguely, the thought of an entire era. Some of those who had earlier expressed the general point of view adopted and sharpened by Paley were John Ray, who had published *The Wisdom of God Manifested in the Works of the Creation* in 1691; William Durham, whose *Physico-Theology* appeared in 1713; and— perhaps most important for *Natural Theology*—the Dutch philosopher Bernard Nieuwentyt (1654-1718) to whose works Paley is heavily indebted for his famous "watch" analogy. Much of the enduring value of Paley consists, then, not in his being "original" but in his being supremely a man of his time, holding the views of his time and expressing them with his own extraordinary skill.

Natural Theology hardly deserves the neglect, then, which it has suffered for the past century. If its true importance was somewhat exaggerated in the half-century or more which followed its publication, so its comparative desuetude since then has been extreme. As long as the argument from design is discussed at all, Paley's statement of the case for it will remain relevant—and to some, perhaps, convincing. At any rate, Paley's admirable clarity in advancing the one theistic argument both respected by severest critics and treasured by simple believers deserves to be heard. The classical teleological argument should not be stated exclusively, today, by its would-be demolishers.

II

Although Paley's writings have unfortunately not been available for many years, one argument concerning "the stone and the watch" has been widely perpetuated in connection with his name. This argument, as will be shown below, was indeed of immense importance to him, but an examination of *Natural Theology* as a whole reveals that there is more to Paley's philosophical position than this often crudely understood analogy.

The argument of *Natural Theology* falls into two major

parts. The first (employing the illustration of the watch) pro-
pounds a proof for the *existence* of the Deity as a cosmic designer; the second attempts a demonstration of the *attributes*
of the designer.

First examining the proof for the Deity's existence, we
should note what *kind* of argument is used. Paley is a convinced empiricist. The basic trustworthiness of sense experience is presupposed, as is the general reliability of memory.
His philosophical method is consistently to adopt the standards accepted in the empirical sciences: he rejects any de-
pendence upon innate ideas, he mistrusts the a priori, he
avoids reliance on any "revelation" claiming immunity from
rigorous criticism. In all this, Paley (like the scientist) claims
not to provide absolute deductive logical necessity for his conclusions, in the manner of Descartes' demand for the indubita-
ble, but rather to offer inductively reasonable grounds for belief in his assertions—grounds sufficient for complete rational
conviction. Paley is aiming, therefore, at building as strong a
probable case as possible; he will be content if he can show
that it would be arbitrary and unreasonable—though not
necessarily self-contradictory—to reject it.

Operating with such a method, how would one ever go
about proving with a high degree of probability the existence
of any designer? Two aspects may be distinguished within the
generalized logic of such a proof. First, one must *observe*
something which possesses the characteristics of design. Without such an observation (which might be provided by the
discovery of a watch) the empirical method is unable to take
its first step. But what, specifically, are the observable characteristics of design? The contrast between watch and stone
supplies Paley's answer. In the watch, unlike the stone, we
find parts which *work together*. More, in thus co-operating the
parts *achieve a common end* (not necessarily an "end" useful
to man, it may be noted) of which, taken separately, they
would be quite incapable. The parts of a watch, for example,
all combine to produce an effect far beyond the power of any
particular spring or cog, namely, to cause "an index, by an

equable and measured progression, to pass over a given space in a given time." [1]

The second aspect of any proof for the existence of a designer is at least recognized, though no doubt insufficiently explored, by Paley. Observation is not enough, no matter how empirical the methodology. In addition to *sensing*, merely, the characteristics of design, one must have the power of *recognizing* them for what they are. And for this, Paley notes, one needs "some previous knowledge of the subject, to perceive and understand it." [2] How such "previous knowledge" is obtained, its degree of reliability, its logical status within a purely empiricist epistemology, its very possibility with respect to inferences from natural objects to a unique cosmic designer *not* "previously" known—these questions are not deeply explored. Such neglect is doubly unfortunate since they were significantly among the questions pressed by Hume in his penetrating critique of the argument from design. But if Paley is seriously vulnerable at this point, he is at least aware of the need for more than observation alone in any empirical proof; and by recognizing that his argument depends on judgment and memory as well as sheer sensation, he raises fruitful issues for inductive methodology.

In sum, then, Paley argues that we are capable both of observing certain characteristics in things and, by an experientially well-grounded analogy between like causes and like effects, of recognizing them to be the unfailing marks of design. The most important of these marks are the co-operation of parts and the resulting production of an end. Wherever we find these phenomena we may reasonably infer that they are the product of deliberate design; that is, he concludes, we may rationally assert the existence of a designer.

Anticipating objections to this argument, Paley clarifies his stand by specifying more precisely what, at this point, he intends to claim. (1) He does *not* need to hold, he insists, either that the object endowed with the characteristics of design

---

must at any time actually be experienced in the process of construction by a designer or, indeed, even that it be capable of being constructed by human efforts. The products of the lost arts of ancient peoples may baffle us today, but we are legitimately confident that we are in the presence of designed objects nonetheless. And (we may interpolate for Paley) if exploration of our solar system should discover, on other planets, machines beyond our power to build, we should be arbitrary and unreasonable to assert, merely because of our impotence, that they were natural formations sufficiently accounted for without reference to the purposes of designers. (2) Moreover, Paley contends that his argument is not damaged if the designed object has redundancies or defects. The intelligence or excellence of the designer is not here at issue; and if enough of the design is recognizable to make possible a verdict even of *poor* workmanship, the existence, at least, of a worker is established. (3) But what of chance? Could one not appeal to randomness alone to account for alleged characteristics of design? Paley agrees that no logical contradiction precludes such an evasion of his argument's conclusion, but he insists that it is arbitrary and unreasonable to appeal to the vastly improbable hypothesis that intelligible order is produced by sheer accident rather than to the more probable hypothesis that such an effect is the product in *all* cases (as it is *observed* to be in some cases) of an intelligent orderer. (4) Similarly, appeal to a "principle of order in things" is an arbitrary attempt to substitute the unknown for the familiar. What grounds in experience, Paley asks, support such a view? Worse, what does such an assertion *mean?* We know what is meant by saying that a *designer* is capable of effecting certain results, but to suppose a *principle* capable of effective activity is unintelligible: in Paley's repeated phrase, "a perversion of language." (5) Precisely the same defense could be used against the supposition that a "natural law," any more than a principle, could engage in activity. Laws of nature, Paley points out, are only descriptive of operations; and real operations require a real operator. If the products of design are lawful and orderly, so much the more evidence is provided for the belief that they are the work of a designer capable at least of recognizing and utilizing the difference between lawful and lawless, orderly and disorderly action. (6) If the designed object were capable of reproducing itself, some might suppose a designer no longer necessary, but, rather, that an "infinite regress" of reproductions could account for the marks of contrivance. Such an appeal, however, offers no lasting rational satisfaction. *Somewhere* the chain of reproductions must be anchored fast to an original designer—whose skill we must admire all the more for the ability to construct things which not only are capable of achieving an end through co-operation of parts but also are able to reproduce themselves. Why must an infinite succession be ended at some point? Because, Paley points out, "a chain composed of an infinite number of links can no more support itself than a chain composed of a finite number of links." [3]

The application of this general argument to the theological case is, as far as Paley can see, perfectly straightforward. The same characteristics which justly prove the existence of a designer for a watch or other contrivance ought also, when found in nature, to convince any rational being about the existence of the Deity as a cosmic designer. And such characteristics of contrivance are found wherever one may cast his eye. Indeed, the eye itself is a splendid instance of design in nature; one which, Paley shows, far surpasses the telescope "in the complexity, subtlety, and curiosity of the mechanism." [4]

There is no need for us to examine in any detail the specific working out of this fundamental argument. Paley multiplies his examples endlessly to drive his point home; but, as he would be the first to concede, all this is not necessary. The argument is cumulative, each natural contrivance swelling the volume of evidence for the existence of the Deity, but each quite sufficient to make the main point alone, if need be. Just as, "if there were but one watch in the world, it would not be less certain that it had a maker," [5] so the various parts of the

[3] P. 9.   [4] P. 13.   [5] Pp. 32-33.

eye, even if considered apart from all the other evidences available, "compose altogether an apparatus, a system of parts, a preparation of means, so manifest in their design, so exquisite in their contrivance, so successful in their issue, so precious, and so infinitely beneficial in their use, as, in my opinion, to bear down all doubt that can be raised upon the subject." [6]

The "subject," thus far, has been restricted to a proof for the *existence* of a designer. But such a proof, even if successful, falls short of demonstrating that this designer may rightly be called *God*. The second part of *Natural Theology* turns to this task. First the nature of this designer must be determined as far as possible; then, if the discovered attributes are identical with those commonly predicated of God, the claims of religion will be on solid footing. The God of religion is traditionally considered to be personal, for example. So much the better! The cosmic designer must also be personal, since the qualities essential to any designer—consciousness, purpose, volition—are, tautologically, what *constitute* personality. If that personality is not visible in a familiar form, what matter? It is illegitimate to insist that the concept "personality" entails any particular sensible characteristics. It may even be in principle, Paley muses, that beings equipped with different senses might be able to perceive "the powers, properties, and substance of spirits." [7] The Deity's imperceptibility, at any rate, is no ground for rejecting his personality.

Further attributes of the designer require redoubled use of the empirical method. Such properties will be determined on the basis of observations made of products of design in nature. Revelation, stooping to the limitations of our finite minds, may be of great value in interpreting God in images always related to us; but fortunately human reason and the empirical method can supplement revelation to provide both independent confirmation for and literal interpretation of such theological terms as "omnipotence," "omniscience," "omnipres-

6 P. 32.   7 Pp. 35-36.

ence," "eternity," "self-existence," "necessary existence," and
"spirituality." As far as natural theology can show, Paley ad-
mits, any of these terms which are not "negatives" must be
admitted to be "superlatives," the use of which is better justified on grounds of religious fervor than on the available evidence. When we say that God is "omnipotent," for example,
the most we can literally mean is:

> that a power which could create such a world as this is must
> be, beyond all comparison, greater than any which we ex-
> perience in ourselves, than any which we observe in other
> visible agents, greater also than any which we can want, for
> our individual protection and preservation, in the Being
> upon whom we depend.[8]

"Omniscience," again, stands for *very great* wisdom, sufficient
to conduct the observed natural order.

But this is enough, Paley feels; especially if the emotional
benefits from using "superlative" language are still available.
After all, "the terms which the piety and the usage of language
have rendered habitual to us may be as proper as any other." [9]

There is no need to follow any further Paley's empirical
interpretation of the other attributes of the Deity; but it is
worthwhile to notice that he claims on the basis of natural
theology a good deal less than much of his language would
suggest. In discussing the unity of God, for example, he ac-
knowledges that his whole argument "goes no further than
to a unity of counsel," [10] i.e., that he has proved no more
"unity" in God than is present in a jury which has reached
its verdict.

The last, and most crucial, attribute discussed in *Natural
Theology* is the question of the Deity's goodness. If a super-
natural being possesses all the other attributes of God but is
without goodness, can he be called *God?* Or must we not term
such a being "Satan" or "Anti-God"? Paley, however, is sure
that the cosmic designer's goodness can be proved from an examination of his handiwork, and in his consequent attempt to

overcome the problem of evil he runs nearly the gamut of traditional solutions: from a form of Leibniz' doctrine of "compossibles" to an anticipation of James's moral activism. His most characteristic emphases, we may note, are on the "joys" of nature's creatures, the subordinate or unintentional role of pain (teeth were designed for eating, not aching; if God had deliberately set out to inflict suffering, how much better a job he could have done!), and the entirely "unnecessary"—thus benevolent—gift of pleasure beyond biological requirement. We smile, but perhaps not without sympathy, when we read Paley's unselfconscious hymn in praise of the delights of the table:

> Why add pleasure to the act of eating; sweetness and relish to food? Why a new and appropriate sense for the perception of the pleasure? Why should the juice of a peach applied to the palate affect the part so differently from what it does when rubbed upon the palm of the hand? This is a constitution which, so far as appears to me, can be resolved into nothing but the pure benevolence of the Creator.[11]

III

One of Paley's critics, tongue in cheek, has noted that the only fault in the book, considered as an instrument of persuasion, is that it is too conclusive. "If there were no hidden flaw in the reasoning, it would be impossible to understand, not only how any should resist, but how anyone should ever have overlooked the demonstration." [12] Paley himself, of course, hopes to anticipate this objection by protesting that philosophers are irrationally offended by a proof "not only popular, but vulgar" and that they, whose minds are "habitually in search of invention and originality," reject the true conclusions because of the "flatness" of common reasons.[13]

11 P. 70.

12 Leslie Stephen, *History of English Thought in the Eighteenth Century* (2nd edn., 2 vols.; London: Smith, Elder, and Co., 1881), I, 408.

13 P. 44.

Such a psychological explanation, however, is hardly sufficient to answer the sharp criticisms directed from a number of sources against the classical teleological argument.

The most obvious (and, for some, conclusive) source of criticism of Paley's position is post-Darwinian biological science. *Natural Theology,* it might be said, was written more than half a century before *The Origin of Species;* the non-teleological mechanism of natural selection was unheard of at the time; so much the worse for Paley, therefore, whose philosophical viewpoint was so quickly—and so utterly—demolished by scientific advance.

In part this criticism is manifestly justified. Paley was wrong in many of his factual beliefs; it would be futile to burke the point. He thought that species are fixed; they are not. He supposed that species never become extinct; they do. He was unaware of the vast evolutionary history of life on our planet. Hume's germinal suggestion of natural selection in the *Dialogues Concerning Natural Religion* went unnoticed and unanswered. A more primitive concept of natural selection was ridiculed. In 1802 Paley was evidently in no mood to make compromises with evolutionary theory; and it is quite certain that if the Archdeacon were suddenly to be thrown into our modern world, he would be immensely disconcerted.

But it is not so certain, as some of his critics might assume, that his discomfiture would persist indefinitely. The relationship between scientific discovery and philosophical theory is a complex one. As soon as Paley had eliminated from his position all sheerly factual errors, he might well present us with a new revised edition of *Natural Theology* without radically altering his central philosophical viewpoint, only now basing the teleological argument (as others have done and are still doing) on the "complexity, subtlety, and curiosity" of the natural laws governing the evolutionary process itself.

Science qua science can and must examine any factual premises used by philosophers, but it is unequipped to contend with philosophical conclusions qua philosophical. Such a task is best accomplished by philosophers themselves, and

criticisms of Paley from the latter source have not been wanting.

First, an apparent logical weakness in Paley's attempted
demonstration of the goodness of God, to choose but one
example, is a confusion, of a type exposed by Hume, between
deriving a conclusion from evidence and arguing that a conclusion (previously held) is *compatible* with the evidence.
Paley's explicit methodology requires that whatever he claims
about God be inductively derived from observation of the
world. But his argument actually seems to operate with quite
a different logic; it is aimed, whatever its success, at showing
that God may be considered good *even though* the evidence
seems to tell against it at a number of points. As Hume, in the
Dialogues Concerning Natural Religion, points out: "I am
sceptic enough to allow that the bad appearances, notwithstanding all my reasonings, may be compatible with such
attributes as you suppose: But surely they can never prove
these attributes." [14]

Paley, of course, is not entirely without a reply to Hume
on this point. He is not, nor does he claim to be, building
theology from the foundations upward. On the contrary,
natural theology is a discipline which finds itself in a world
which has for centuries listened to the assertions of revealed
theology concerning the nature of God. In such a world it is
hardly possible to pretend, as Hume does, that theological
investigations will be carried on as though no one had ever
conceived of God as infinitely good. Given this situation, revealed theology, within Paley's methodology, provides the
hypothesis that God is good; natural theology supplies (1)
empirical data which tend to verify the hypothesis and (2)
theoretical considerations which serve to show why other data
do not conclusively falsify the hypothesis. Hume's criticism at
this point not only overlooks the methodological role of
natural theology as seen by its practitioners but also fails to
recognize the legitimate importance of the hypothetical move-

14 David Hume, *Dialogues Concerning Natural Religion,* "Library of
Liberal Arts," No. 174 (New York: Liberal Arts Press, 1962), p. 211.

ment of thought within empirical methodology in general. He seems to presuppose a Baconian approach, long since abandoned by scientists, to the process of "deriving" conclusions from facts. We have noticed that Paley, on the other hand, is aware of the role of intelligent judgment in inductive thinking as an indispensable complement to sheer observation. However much we may disagree with Paley's answer to the problem of evil, it will be on other grounds, then, than the Humean attack on logical procedure.

Paley's treatment of the question of infinite regress, secondly, suffers from uncritical reliance on an analogy. When he dismisses any appeal to infinite regress on the ground that an infinite chain is no more self-supporting than a finite chain, he has fallen into the errors (1) of picturing causal sequence under the model of a material chain and (2) of imagining the difference between "infinite" and "finite" to be the difference between a long chain and a still longer one. But this clearly is not adequate. Does the whole, if infinite, even constitute something that *needs* support? Even if we were to accept Paley's unfortunate comparison between temporal, causal sequence and a chain, for the sake of argument, would it make sense to ask whether a really infinite chain (*per impossibile*) were supported or falling? Would there be any difference between a "supported" and a "uniformly falling" infinite chain if that chain constituted all reality?

Criticize as we must, Paley's aversion to infinite regress as a putative explanation for particular phenomena was still not foolishness. His way of expressing the objection was inept, to be sure, but the fact remains that infinite regress is not so much an explanation as a rejection of the demand for an explanation. And as such it poses a mortal threat to scientific as well as metaphysical investigation. Both metaphysics and science exist within, depend upon, man's questing, curious impulses; and appeal to infinite regress is, if successful, curiosity's assassin. The mind may be hypnotized into passivity by staring back, and back, and back . . . into the endless depths of time, but this is no way to obtain a sufficient explanation for any specific question. The kind of problems raised by Paley may be muffled in the folds of infinite regress only at the risk of suffocating science as well. The question remains, of course, whether Paley's alternative appeal to a Deity genuinely affords a more satisfying "explanation" for the curious, or a more permanent resting place for the weary. He has at the very least offered a familiar analogy in place of the wholly elusive or the blankly arbitrary. But to what extent does such an offering meet our requirements for an explanation? What, in any event, constitutes an adequate explanation—or a fit analogy—at this level of generality? Paley's answer, it would seem, should be taken more as a stimulus to further hard thinking than as a formula by which to solve all problems.

This need for continued rigorous thought is illustrated, thirdly, by the fact that Paley's entire argument is jeopardized by the query asked by both Hume and Kant: to what extent is the analogy between products of nature and those of human contrivance a legitimate one? Can it possibly be proper to stretch this similarity to the point where it must support the whole rambling superstructure of theology? Are not other analogies—between the universe and, say, a living organism or the product of a cosmic spider's weaving—equally justified (or at least no more greatly strained), lacking only in the power to undergird prior belief in a personal Deity? If so, on what independent ground does one choose as Paley does, rather than as Hume's Philo suggests in Parts V, VI, and VII of the *Dialogues Concerning Natural Religion?*

Here we are once again in a position where "judgment," not observation alone, must determine the answer. In Paley's favor it should be remembered that Kant himself, attacking the argument from design in the *Critique of Pure Reason,* goes as far as to say:

> . . . we are willing to admit, nevertheless, that if we have to name such a cause [for natural "contrivances"], we cannot do better than to follow the analogy of such productions of human design, which are the only ones of which we know completely both cause and effect. There would be

no excuse, if reason were to surrender a causality which it knows, and have recourse to obscure and indemonstrable principles of explanation, which it does not know.[15]

Paley's reasoning is along identical lines. Reliance on the analogy between products of nature and man-made contrivances is justified, he insists, by "uniform experience."

> We see intelligence constantly contriving; that is, we see intelligence constantly producing effects, marked and distinguished by certain properties . . . such as relation to an end, relation of parts to one another and to a common purpose. We see, wherever we are witnesses to the actual formation of things, nothing except intelligence producing effects so marked and distinguished in the same manner. We wish to account for their origin. Our experience suggests a cause perfectly adequate to this account. No experience, no single instance or example, can be offered in favor of any other.[16]

The assertion that the analogy based on intelligence is the *only* experientially justified one as against Philo's superfecundity of alternatives (and particularly against the alternative of sheer, unconscious "generation"), is stoutly maintained by Paley in one of the most thoughtful replies ever given to Hume's attack on this point. "Generation" is the word for a process which *itself* is problematical in a universe not guided by a cosmic intelligence, says Paley. And if the term is expanded to cover the origin of the whole world (as Hume seems inclined to do), the hypothesis loses its intelligibility unless "generation" in its new sense is given a specific use. Without such careful definition, the suggestion is no more than a red herring, distracting our minds from the one empirically meaningful hypothesis in our possession, intelligence, without offering any significant alternative.

> If the term generation signify something quite different from what it signifies on ordinary occasions, it may by the

same latitude signify anything. In which case, a word or phrase taken from the language of Otaheite would convey as much theory concerning the origin of the universe, as it does to talk of its being generated.[17]

Finally, theologians no less than philosophers are among those who can "resist" Paley's arguments. Precisely at the points where Paley defends himself against philosophical attack by capitulating in advance to possible criticism, he opens himself to criticism from the orthodox. When Paley implicitly refuses to violate Hume's principle that causes must be proportioned to their effects (that is, that it is illegitimate "to ascribe to the cause any qualities, but what are exactly sufficient to produce the effect" [18]), he has made the theologically fatal move which prevents him from accepting any "superlative" attributes as literally descriptive of God. And this, in turn, requires that he reinterpret "infinite" as "very, very [unimaginably] great"—but still finite, as far as the interests and requirements of traditional theism are concerned.

One of Kant's criticisms of the teleological argument is also evaded by Paley, but again at a heavy theological price. Kant points out the illegitimacy of the leap from the finite, empirical realm, where evidence of design is found, to the concept of the "absolute totality" of the Supreme Being's alleged existence.[19] But Paley never makes such a leap! His Deity remains, in principle, in the finite order where all the notions of space, time, cause, and even perception, remain applicable. The Deity may, as a matter of fact, be invisible to our eyes, but this is only an inconvenient matter of practice, not something that in principle reflects a wholly different order of being. Paley at times writes as though he would not think us farfetched if we imagined an instrument which

17 Pp. 43-44.

18 David Hume, *An Inquiry Concerning Human Understanding,* "Library of Liberal Arts," No. 49 (New York: Liberal Arts Press, 1955), p. 145.

19 *Critique of Pure Reason,* pp. 263-64.

might detect God's presence, analogous to gravitation or magnetism, in the world around us.[20] But such a finite, almost
material, being (it might be objected) is far from the Lord of
Heaven and Earth of the Bible. His image is more accurately
reflected in the form of eighteenth-century man. "God," remarks one commentator, "has been civilised like man; he has
become scientific and ingenious; he is superior to Watt or
Priestley in devising mechanical contrivances, and is, therefore,
made in the image of that generation of which Watt and
Priestley were conspicuous lights." [21]

Such a line of criticism would no doubt be just, from an
orthodox theological point of view, if Paley had attempted to
replace revelation with his own limited results. It should not
be overlooked, however, that such was not his expressed aim.
On the contrary, his hope—as stated in his own concluding
chapter of *Natural Theology*—was to provide limited confirmation for a Christian religion which was in no way to be
confined to the bare conclusions he supposed himself able to
demonstrate. The concept of God which could emerge from
the application of Paley's empirical methods would inevitably
be a desiccated one; but Paley was of the apparently sincere
opinion that a proof for the existence of even this poor an
approximation of the holy God of Christianity was a step
toward a strengthened confidence in invisible reality, consequently in the possibility of divine revelation, hence in the
truthfulness of the Bible and, ultimately, in the full Christian
God. Paley's *Natural Theology* may not be "religiously satisfying" in itself, but there is no evidence that its author was
hoping to reduce religion to its compass. Paley was not a
passionate man, yet one must remember that he lived in an
age which discouraged "enthusiasm" in religious expression.
We would be unjust to condemn him for being in this way,
as in so many others, a representative of his century.

[20] See above, p. xviii.
[21] Leslie Stephen, *History of English Thought in the Eighteenth Century*, I, 411.

IV

The position represented by Paley is no longer popular, his arguments are no longer generally persuasive. Both philosophy and theology have tended to reject Paley's alternative to sheer skepticism or dogmatic fideism on issues of religion. Thus at the very least Paley continues to illuminate the philosophical and theological scene by posing a contrast, vividly and well, to the contemporary majority view. But Paley's *Natural Theology* provides us with more than this; it remains the best statement of what is generally recognized as the most highly respected theistic argument in its classical form. Paley himself claims that rejection of his argument would demand "the inference not only that the present order of nature is insufficient to prove the existence of an intelligent Creator, but that no imaginable order would be sufficient to prove it. . . ." [22]

There are many today who insist that this "inference," which Paley rejects as unthinkable, is manifestly justified. The most radical twentieth-century argument in support of such a critical stand has maintained that all metaphysical utterances—and thus all of Paley's attempts to make assertions about an unobservable designer who is alleged to be responsible for the observable order of the universe—fail to satisfy the standards of literal significance and are consequently devoid of any meaning (beyond certain emotional effects that may be produced or expressed through factually empty verbiage). But, although some continue to support this position, which makes argument against detailed points unnecessary and irrelevant by sweeping away at one stroke all of natural theology as "literally senseless," contemporary philosophers have on the whole now withdrawn from this view. Despite the appeal of its evident simplicity, vigor, and directness, this "short way" with metaphysics has come to be recognized as too vulnerably dependent on an a priori criterion of meaning— and, therefore, as too imperfectly empirical to satisfy the very empiricists who had hoped to employ it. The current mood

22 P. 38.

among philosophers tends to be much more cautious and *ad hoc:* each argument, it is generally conceded, needs examination on its own merits. And in this climate Paley's famous argument is no less deserving of attention than many others.

Nevertheless, suspicion still lingers in many quarters—among both philosophers and theologians—that a position like Paley's (though meaningful) is somehow *in principle* misconceived. The source of this opinion seems to be a prevailing assumption that religious belief is utterly, necessarily, and properly irrelevant to empirical fact. Criticism of such a bald assumption, however, may be expected in current discussion.

First, there will need to be a fresh reminder of an often overlooked fact, namely, that empirical discoveries *have,* without question, enormously influenced religious belief over the years. Such influences, leading sometimes to the radical alterations of beliefs (as when discovery of the facts of evolution forced the withdrawal of certain untenable interpretations of Genesis) and sometimes even to recasting prevailing ideas about the nature and purposes of God (as when the events surrounding the upheavals of World Wars I and II occasioned the general abandonment of optimistic theologies of progress) —such influences are awkward facts to explain, on the supposition that religious belief and empirical fact are irrelevant to one another. Still, it may be countered, these influences may be accounted for as merely *psychologically* based. One seems forced to admit that religious belief and empirical facts are not "utterly" sealed off from one another in every way; but Paley's argument (like all others of its type) presupposes not merely a psychological but a *logical* relevance of empirical fact to religious belief. Theological claims, however, because of their notorious incapacity for being clearly falsified by any specified set of particular occurrences or nonoccurrences (so the objection may run), cannot be supposed to share this logical kind of relevance with the empirical hypotheses of the natural sciences.

But, secondly, a modern reply to this qualified restatement of the "irrelevance" thesis might begin by pointing out, as philosophers of science have increasingly been doing, that the very pronouncements of the natural scientist have proved, upon analysis, to admit widely different degrees of amenability to direct empirical verification or falsification. Although always remaining logically relevant to empirical fact, some scientific statements of foundational theoretical status may be "unfalsifiable" by any of the means relevant to the testing of lower-level experimental hypotheses in the sciences. Thus it may turn out that those now arguing against the viability of natural theology, on the basis of an alleged "necessary" (logical) irrelevance of religious and metaphysical claims to the facts of experience, are basing their argument on an overly simple understanding of "relevance"—a notion gained from neglecting the logical complexities of empirical science as well as of theological discourse. Be this as it may, it is at least evident that nothing is to be gained from attempting an assimilation of high-generality, or "key," theological statements, like Paley's, to low-generality, or "derivative," hypotheses within the sciences, and then professing surprise at the failure of the two types of statements to manifest the same logical behavior. Thus, though Paley himself tends to neglect these logical refinements in his eagerness to show the bearing of fact upon religious belief, his modern sympathizers—without in the least abandoning his aims—will no doubt look more to the higher reaches of scientific theories and models for hints about the character of the logical relevance of theological statements to the empirical world.

Moreover, the thesis of logical "irrelevance" between religious belief and the world of experience must deal with the notorious fact that apparent *disorder* and lack of benevolent design in the world have always been understood as an *obstacle* to belief in a Deity such as is argued for by Paley. But this must work both ways: if the problem of evil is logically relevant to the *dis*confirmation of theological affirmations, as is still widely insisted on by critics of religious belief, then religious belief is not irrelevant to empirical fact—and natural theology as an enterprise is legitimate, at least, though its specific arguments and conclusions may perhaps be mistaken. Further, if there can in principle be evidence against a belief, then there can in principle be evidence in its favor. Against disorder, discovery of order is significant; and to understand the logical point of Paley's appeal to the amount of pleasure in the universe, we need only compare complaints about the amount of suffering which may also be found. The skeptic may not in good logic scorn as "irrelevant" the evidences offered in support of religious belief, while himself pointing to other empirical facts as damaging to the possibility of a rationally responsible religion.

Thirdly, we must recognize that it is not only the skeptic who frequently maintains the "irrelevance" thesis today. Theologians, as well, have accepted it as shelter against the uprooting winds of scientific revolution. But current discussion is likely to make clear that total abandonment of the position represented broadly by Paley can lead only to still more profound "uprooting." Unless religious belief is kept relevant— at some level—to the empirical world, it cannot fail to evaporate into a purely subjective adjunct to poetry and ethics. Perhaps this is a prospect which fails to disturb some modern theologians, though it involves the abdication of religion's concern for wholeness of truth, including truth about the world, and leads to a neglect of historic doctrines of creation and providence; but for Paley and his present-day sympathizers such an outcome would rob religion of most of its importance and would soon undermine even its waning power to sustain interest in its imagery or its ethos.

This Introduction is not a suitable place in which to attempt a settlement of such great questions; its aim, rather, has been to encourage further discussion of the issues Paley continues to raise. Even if the argument from design is ultimately found wanting, as it no doubt must be in Paley's pre-evolutionary expression of it, the Archdeacon of Carlisle remains an important figure. In him we find a man who, right or wrong in his specific views, refused to isolate reason and religion from one another. He shows us that it is possible to

discuss theological belief without abandoning a constant concern for the relevance of empirical fact, without forgoing
rigorous dedication to standards of logical consistency and
the canons of argument in general, and without sacrificing a
singular clarity of style. We can no longer believe precisely
what he believed nor argue precisely as he argued; but we can
honor his goals and his achievements by attempting ourselves
to realize whatever in them may be enduring.

FREDERICK FERRÉ

Dickinson College
Carlisle, Pennsylvania
March, 1963

SELECTED BIBLIOGRAPHY

READINGS ON THE TELEOLOGICAL ARGUMENT

HUME, DAVID. *An Enquiry Concerning Human Understanding.* London, 1748. Section 11.

———. *Dialogues Concerning Natural Religion.* London, 1779.

KANT, IMMANUEL. *Critique of Pure Reason.* Riga, 1781. "Transcendental Dialectic," Book II, Chapter 3, Section 6.

———. *Critique of Judgment.* Berlin, 1790. Part II.

BERGSON, HENRI. *Creative Evolution.* Tr. A. MITCHELL. New York: Henry Holt and Co., 1911.

MORGAN, C. LLOYD. *Emergent Evolution.* 2 vols. London: Williams and Norgate, 1923.

TENNANT, F. R. *Philosophical Theology.* 2 vols. Cambridge: Cambridge University Press, 1930.

LECOMTE DU NOÜY, P. *Human Destiny.* London, New York, Toronto: Longmans, Green and Co., 1947.

SIMPSON, GEORGE GAYLORD. *The Meaning of Evolution.* New Haven: Yale University Press, 1949.

BERTOCCI, PETER ANTHONY. *Introduction to the Philosophy of Religion.* New York: Prentice-Hall, Inc., 1951. Chapters 11-15.

DUCASSE, C. J. *A Philosophical Scrutiny of Religion.* New York: Ronald Press Co., 1953. Chapter 15.

HOSPERS, JOHN. *An Introduction to Philosophical Analysis.* New York: Prentice-Hall, Inc., 1953. Chapter 5.

TEILHARD DE CHARDIN, PIERRE. *The Phenomenon of Man.* Tr. B. WALL. New York: Harper & Bros., 1959.

READINGS ON WILLIAM PALEY

STEPHEN, LESLIE. *History of English Thought in the Eight-*

eenth Century. 2nd edn., 2 vols. London: Smith, Elder, and Co., 1881.

ALBEE, ERNEST. *A History of English Utilitarianism.* New York: Macmillan Co., 1902.

SORLEY, W. R. *A History of English Philosophy.* New York: G. P. Putnam's Sons, 1921.

We perceive - that the watch

it's several parts are framed and put
together for a purpose - there forked
and adjusted as to produce motion

Paley describing each motion or
function of each part in a watch

[Finding a watch on the ground]

December 2005   February 2006
S M T W T F S   S M T W T F S
          1 2 3   1 2 3 4
4 5 6 7 8 9 10   5 6 7 8 9 10 11
11 12 13 14 15 16 17   12 13 14 15 16 17 18
18 19 20 21 22 23 24   19 20 21 22 23 24 25
25 26 27 28 29 30 31   26 27 28

Thursday, January 12   353

13

| 7:00 |
| 7:30 |
| 8:00 |
| 8:30 |
| 9:00 |
| 9:30 |
| 10:00 |
| 10:30 |
| 11:00 |
| 11:30 |
| 12:00 |
| 12:30 |
| 1:00 |
| 1:30 |
| 2:00 |
| 2:30 |
| 3:00 |
| 3:30 |
| 4:00 |
| 4:30 |
| 5:00 |

NOTE ON THE TEXT

The present edition of selections from Paley's *Natural Theology* is taken from the American Tract Society text (New York, n. d.), which was widely used in American colleges and seminaries during the second quarter of the nineteenth century and which is a faithful rendering of Paley's original London edition (1802).

The present edition is abridged. The Table of Contents, however, is complete; bracketed material there indicates sections omitted in the text. Additional footnotes supplied by the editor are also bracketed. Paley's original text has been unaltered except for punctuation and spelling, which have been made to conform to modern American usage. An Index has also been added by the editor.

NATURAL THEOLOGY

CHAPTER ONE

STATE OF THE ARGUMENT

In crossing a heath, suppose I pitched my foot against a *stone* and were asked how the stone came to be there, I might possibly answer that for anything I knew to the contrary it had lain there forever; nor would it, perhaps, be very easy to show the absurdity of this answer. But suppose I had found a *watch* upon the ground, and it should be inquired how the watch happened to be in that place, I should hardly think of the answer which I had before given, that for anything I knew the watch might have always been there. Yet why should not this answer serve for the watch as well as for the stone; why is it not as admissible in the second case as in the first? For this reason, and for no other, namely, that when we come to inspect the watch, we perceive—what we could not discover in the stone—that its several parts are framed and put together for a purpose, e.g., that they are so formed and adjusted as to produce motion, and that motion so regulated as to point out the hour of the day; that if the different parts had been differently shaped from what they are, or placed after any other manner or in any other order than that in which they are placed, either no motion at all would have been carried on in the machine, or none which would have answered the use that is now served by it. To reckon up a few of the plainest of these parts and of their offices, all tending to one result: we see a cylindrical box containing a coiled elastic spring, which, by its endeavor to relax itself, turns round the box. We next observe a flexible chain—artificially wrought for the sake of flexure—communicating the action of the spring from the box to the fusee. We then find a series of wheels, the teeth of which catch in and apply to each other, conducting the motion from the fusee to the balance and from the balance to the pointer, and at the same time, by the size and shape of those wheels, so regulating that motion as to terminate in causing an index, by an equable and measured progression, to pass over a given space in a given time. We take notice that the wheels are made of brass, in order to keep them from rust; the springs of steel, no other metal being so elastic; that over the face of the watch there is placed a glass, a material employed in no other part of the work, but in the room of which, if there had been any other than a transparent substance, the hour could not be seen without opening the case. This mechanism being observed—it requires indeed an examination of the instrument, and perhaps some previous knowledge of the subject, to perceive and understand it; but being once, as we have said, observed and understood—the inference we think is inevitable, that the watch must have had a maker—that there must have existed, at some time and at some place or other, an artificer or artificers who formed it for the purpose which we find it actually to answer, who completely comprehended its construction and designed its use.

I. Nor would it, I apprehend, weaken the conclusion, that we had never seen a watch made—that we had never known an artist capable of making one—that we were altogether incapable of executing such a piece of workmanship ourselves, or of understanding in what manner it was performed; all this being no more than what is true of some exquisite remains of ancient art, of some lost arts, and, to the generality of mankind, of the more curious productions of modern manufacture. Does one man in a million know how oval frames are turned? Ignorance of this kind exalts our opinion of the unseen and unknown artist's skill, if he be unseen and unknown, but raises no doubt in our minds of the existence and agency of such an artist, at some former time and in some place or other. Nor can I perceive that it varies at all the inference, whether the question arise concerning a human agent or concerning an agent of a different species, or an agent possessing in some respects a different nature.

II. Neither, secondly, would it invalidate our conclusion,

that the watch sometimes went wrong or that it seldom went exactly right. The purpose of the machinery, the design, and the designer might be evident, and in the case supposed, would be evident, in whatever way we accounted for the irregularity of the movement, or whether we could account for it or not. It is not necessary that a machine be perfect in order to show with what design it was made: still less necessary, where the only question is whether it were made with any design at all.

III. Nor, thirdly, would it bring any uncertainty into the argument, if there were a few parts of the watch, concerning which we could not discover or had not yet discovered in what manner they conduced to the general effect; or even some parts, concerning which we could not ascertain whether they conduced to that effect in any manner whatever. For, as to the first branch of the case, if by the loss, or disorder, or decay of the parts in question, the movement of the watch were found in fact to be stopped, or disturbed, or retarded, no doubt would remain in our minds as to the utility or intention of these parts, although we should be unable to investigate the manner according to which, or the connection by which, the ultimate effect depended upon their action or assistance; and the more complex the machine, the more likely is this obscurity to arise. Then, as to the second thing supposed, namely, that there were parts which might be spared without prejudice to the movement of the watch, and that we had proved this by experiment, these superfluous parts, even if we were completely assured that they were such, would not vacate the reasoning which we had instituted concerning other parts. The indication of contrivance remained, with respect to them, nearly as it was before.

IV. Nor, fourthly, would any man in his senses think the existence of the watch with its various machinery accounted for, by being told that it was one out of possible combinations of material forms; that whatever he had found in the place where he found the watch, must have contained some internal configuration or other; and that this configuration might be the structure now exhibited, namely, of the works of a watch, as well as a different structure.

V. Nor, fifthly, would it yield his inquiry more satisfaction, to be answered that there existed in things a principle of order, which had disposed the parts of the watch into their present form and situation. He never knew a watch made by the principle of order; nor can he even form to himself an idea of what is meant by a principle of order distinct from the intelligence of the watchmaker.

VI. Sixthly, he would be surprised to hear that the mechanism of the watch was no proof of contrivance, only a motive to induce the mind to think so:

VII. And not less surprised to be informed that the watch in his hand was nothing more than the result of the laws of *metallic* nature. It is a perversion of language to assign any law as the efficient, operative cause of any thing. A law presupposes an agent, for it is only the mode according to which an agent proceeds: it implies a power, for it is the order according to which that power acts. Without this agent, without this power, which are both distinct from itself, the *law* does nothing, is nothing. The expression, "the law of metallic nature," may sound strange and harsh to a philosophic ear; but it seems quite as justifiable as some others which are more familiar to him, such as "the law of vegetable nature," "the law of animal nature," or, indeed, as "the law of nature" in general, when assigned as the cause of phenomena, in exclusion of agency and power, or when it is substituted into the place of these.

VIII. Neither, lastly, would our observer be driven out of his conclusion or from his confidence in its truth by being told that he knew nothing at all about the matter. He knows enough for his argument; he knows the utility of the end; he knows the subserviency and adaptation of the means to the end. These points being known, his ignorance of other points, his doubts concerning other points affect not the certainty of his reasoning. The consciousness of knowing little need not beget a distrust of that which he does know.

CHAPTER TWO

STATE OF THE ARGUMENT CONTINUED

Suppose, in the next place, that the person who found the watch should after some time discover that, in addition to all the properties which he had hitherto observed in it, it possessed the unexpected property of producing in the course of its movement another watch like itself—the thing is conceivable; that it contained within it a mechanism, a system of parts—a mold, for instance, or a complex adjustment of lathes, files, and other tools—evidently and separately calculated for this purpose; let us inquire what effect ought such a discovery to have upon his former conclusion.

I. The first effect would be to increase his admiration of the contrivance, and his conviction of the consummate skill of the contriver. Whether he regarded the object of the contrivance, the distinct apparatus, the intricate, yet in many parts intelligible mechanism by which it was carried on, he would perceive in this new observation nothing but an additional reason for doing what he had already done—for referring the construction of the watch to design and to supreme art. If that construction *without* this property, or, which is the same thing, before this property had been noticed, proved intention and art to have been employed about it, still more strong would the proof appear when he came to the knowledge of this further property, the crown and perfection of all the rest.

II. He would reflect that, though the watch before him were *in some sense* the maker of the watch which was fabricated in the course of its movements, yet it was in a very different sense from that in which a carpenter, for instance, is the maker of a chair—the author of its contrivance, the cause of the relation of its parts to their use. With respect to these, the first watch was no cause at all to the second; in no such sense as this was it the author of the constitution and order, either of the parts which the new watch contained, or of the parts by the aid and instrumentality of which it was produced. We might possibly say, but with great latitude of expression, that a stream of water ground corn; but no latitude of expression would allow us to say, no stretch of conjecture could lead us to think that the stream of water built the mill, though it were too ancient for us to know who the builder was. What the stream of water does in the affair is neither more nor less than this: by the application of an unintelligent impulse to a mechanism previously arranged, arranged independently of it and arranged by intelligence, an effect is produced, namely, the corn is ground. But the effect results from the arrangement. The force of the stream cannot be said to be the cause or the author of the effect, still less of the arrangement. Understanding and plan in the formation of the mill were not the less necessary for any share which the water has in grinding the corn; yet is this share the same as that which the watch would have contributed to the production of the new watch, upon the supposition assumed in the last section. Therefore,

III. Though it be now no longer probable that the individual watch which our observer had found was made immediately by the hand of an artificer, yet this alteration does not in anywise affect the inference that an artificer had been originally employed and concerned in the production. The argument from design remains as it was. Marks of design and contrivance are no more accounted for now than they were before. In the same thing, we may ask for the cause of different properties. We may ask for the cause of the color of a body, of its hardness, of its heat; and these causes may be all different. We are now asking for the cause of that subserviency to a use, that relation to an end, which we have remarked in the watch before us. No answer is given to this question by telling us that a preceding watch produced it. There cannot be design without a designer; contrivance without a contriver; order without choice; arrangement without anything capable of arranging; subserviency and relation to a purpose without that which could intend a purpose; means suitable to an end, and executing their office in accomplishing that end, without the end ever having been contemplated or the means accommodated to it. Arrangement, disposition of parts, subserviency of means to an end, relation of instruments to a use imply the presence of intelligence and mind. No one, therefore, can rationally believe that the insensible, inanimate watch, from which the watch before us issued, was the proper cause of the mechanism we so much admire in it—could be truly said to have constructed the instrument, disposed its parts, assigned their office, determined their order, action, and mutual dependency, combined their several motions into one result, and that also a result connected with the utilities of other beings. All these properties, therefore, are as much unaccounted for as they were before.

IV. Nor is anything gained by running the difficulty farther back, that is, by supposing the watch before us to have been produced from another watch, that from a former, and so on indefinitely. Our going back ever so far brings us no nearer to the least degree of satisfaction upon the subject. Contrivance is still unaccounted for. We still want a contriver. A designing mind is neither supplied by this supposition nor dispensed with. If the difficulty were diminished the farther we went back, by going back indefinitely we might exhaust it. And this is the only case to which this sort of reasoning applies. Where there is a tendency, or, as we increase the number of terms, a continual approach toward a limit, *there,* by supposing the number of terms to be what is called infinite, we may conceive the limit to be attained; but where there is no such tendency or approach, nothing is effected by lengthening the series. There is no difference as to the point in question, whatever there may be as to many points, between one series and another—between a series which is finite and a series which is infinite. A chain composed of an infinite number of links can no more support itself than a chain composed of a finite number of links. And of this we are assured, though we never *can* have tried the experiment; because, by increasing the number of links, from ten, for instance, to a hundred, from a hundred to a thousand, etc., we make not the smallest approach, we observe not the smallest tendency toward self-support. There is no difference in this respect—yet there may be a great difference in several respects—between a chain of a greater or less length, between one chain and another, between one that is finite and one that is infinite. This very much resembles the case before us. The machine which we are inspecting demonstrates, by its construction, contrivance and design. Contrivance must have had a contriver, design a designer, whether the machine immediately proceeded from another machine or not. That circumstance alters not the case. That other machine may, in like manner, have proceeded from a former machine: nor does that alter the case; the contrivance must have had a contriver. That former one from one preceding it: no alteration still; a contriver is still necessary. No tendency is perceived, no approach toward a diminution of this necessity. It is the same with any and every succession of these machines—a succession of ten, of a hundred, of a thousand; with one series, as with another—a series which is finite, as with a series which is infinite. In whatever other respects they may differ, in this they do not. In all equally, contrivance and design are unaccounted for.

The question is not simply, how came the first watch into existence?—which question, it may be pretended, is done away by supposing the series of watches thus produced from one another to have been infinite, and consequently to have had no such *first* for which it was necessary to provide a cause. This, perhaps, would have been nearly the state of the question, if nothing had been before us but an unorganized, unmechanized substance, without mark or indication of contrivance. It might be difficult to show that such substance could not have existed from eternity, either in succession—if it were possible, which I think it is not, for unorganized bodies to spring from one another—or by individual perpetuity. But that is not the question now. To suppose it to be so is to suppose that it made no difference whether he had found a watch or a stone.

As it is, the metaphysics of that question have no place; for, in the watch which we are examining are seen contrivance, design, an end, a purpose, means for the end, adaptation to the purpose. And the question which irresistibly presses upon our thoughts is, whence this contrivance and design? The thing required is the intending mind, the adapted hand, the intelligence by which that hand was directed. This question, this demand is not shaken off by increasing a number or succession of substances destitute of these properties; nor the more, by increasing that number to infinity. If it be said that, upon the supposition of one watch being produced from another in the course of that other's movements and by means of the mechanism within it, we have a cause for the watch in my hand, namely, the watch from which it proceeded; I deny that for the design, the contrivance, the suitableness of means to an end, the adaptation of instruments to a use, all of which we discover in the watch, we have any cause whatever. It is in vain, therefore, to assign a series of such causes or to allege that a series may be carried back to infinity; for I do not admit that we have yet any cause at all for the phenomena, still less any series of causes either finite or infinite. Here is contrivance but no contriver; proofs of design, but no designer.

V. Our observer would further also reflect that the maker of the watch before him was in truth and reality the maker of every watch produced from it: there being no difference, except that the latter manifests a more exquisite skill, between the making of another watch with his own hands, by the mediation of files, lathes, chisels, etc., and the disposing, fixing, and inserting of these instruments, or of others equivalent to them, in the body of the watch already made, in such a manner as to form a new watch in the course of the movements which he had given to the old one. It is only working by one set of tools instead of another.

The conclusion which the *first* examination of the watch, of its works, construction, and movement, suggested, was that it must have had, for cause and author of that construction, an artificer who understood its mechanism and designed its use. This conclusion is invincible. A *second* examination presents us with a new discovery. The watch is found, in the course of its movement, to produce another watch similar to itself; and not only so, but we perceive in it a system or organization separately calculated for that purpose. What effect would this discovery have or ought it to have upon our former inference? What, as has already been said, but to increase beyond measure our admiration of the skill which had been employed in the formation of such a machine? Or shall it, instead of this, all at once turn us round to an opposite conclusion, namely, that no art or skill whatever has been concerned in the business, although all other evidences of art and skill remain as they were, and this last and supreme piece of art be now added to the rest? Can this be maintained without absurdity? Yet this is atheism.

CHAPTER THREE

APPLICATION OF THE ARGUMENT

This is atheism; for every indication of contrivance, every manifestation of design which existed in the watch, exists in the works of nature, with the difference on the side of nature of being greater and more, and that in a degree which exceeds all computation. I mean that the contrivances of nature surpass the contrivances of art in the complexity, subtlety, and curiosity of the mechanism; and still more, if possible, do they go beyond them in number and variety; yet, in a multitude of cases, are not less evidently mechanical, not less evidently contrivances, not less evidently accommodated to their end or suited to their office than are the most perfect productions of human ingenuity.

I know no better method of introducing so large a subject than that of comparing a single thing with a single thing: an eye, for example, with a telescope. As far as the examination of the instrument goes, there is precisely the same proof that the eye was made for vision as there is that the telescope was made for assisting it. They are made upon the same principles, both being adjusted to the laws by which the transmission and refraction of rays of light are regulated. I speak not of the origin of the laws themselves; but such laws being fixed, the construction in both cases is adapted to them. For instance, these laws require, in order to produce the same effect, that rays of light in passing from water into the eye should be refracted by a more convex surface than when it passes out of air into the eye. Accordingly, we find that the eye of a fish, in that part of it called the crystalline lens, is much rounder than the eye of terrestrial animals. What plainer manifestation of design can there be than this difference? What could a mathematical instrument maker have done more to show his knowledge of his principle, his application of that knowledge, his suiting of his means to his end—I will not say to display the compass or excellence of his skill and art, for in these all comparison is indecorous, but to testify counsel, choice, consideration, purpose?

To some it may appear a difference sufficient to destroy all similitude between the eye and the telescope, that the one is a perceiving organ, the other an unperceiving instrument. The fact is that they are both instruments. And as to the mechanism, at least as to the mechanism being employed, and even as to the kind of it, this circumstance varies not the analogy at all. For observe what the constitution of the eye is. It is necessary, in order to produce distinct vision, that an image or picture of the object be formed at the bottom of the eye. Whence this necessity arises, or how the picture is connected with the sensation or contributes to it, it may be difficult, nay, we will confess, if you please, impossible for us to search out. But the present question is not concerned in the inquiry. It may be true that in this and in other instances we trace mechanical contrivance a certain way, and that then we come to something which is not mechanical, or which is inscrutable. But this affects not the certainty of our investigation, as far as we have gone. The difference between an animal and an automatic statue consists in this, that in the animal we trace the mechanism to a certain point, and then we are stopped, either the mechanism being too subtle for our discernment, or something else beside the known laws of mechanism taking place; whereas, in the automaton, for the comparatively few motions of which it is capable, we trace the mechanism throughout. But, up to the limit, the reasoning is as clear and certain in the one case as in the other. In the example before us it is a matter of certainty, because it is a matter which experience and observation demonstrate, that the formation of an image at the bottom of the eye is necessary to perfect vision. The formation then of such an image being necessary—no matter how —to the sense of sight and to the exercise of that sense, the apparatus by which it is formed is constructed and put together not only with infinitely more art, but upon the selfsame principles of art as in the telescope or the camera obscura. The perception arising from the image may be laid out of the question; for the production of the image, these are instruments of the same kind. The end is the same, the means are the same. The purpose in both is alike, the contrivance for accomplishing that purpose is in both alike. The lenses of the telescopes and humors of the eye bear a complete resemblance to one another, in their figure, their position, and in their power over the rays of light, namely, in bringing each pencil to a point at the right distance from the lens; namely, in the eye, at the exact place where the membrane is spread to receive it. How is it possible, under circumstances of such close affinity, and under the operation of equal evidence, to exclude contrivance from the one, yet to acknowledge the proof of contrivance having been employed, as the plainest and clearest of all propositions, in the other?

The resemblance between the two cases is still more accurate, and obtains in more points than we have yet represented, or than we are, on the first view of the subject, aware of. In dioptric telescopes there is an imperfection of this nature. Pencils of light in passing through glass lenses are separated into different colors, thereby tinging the object, especially the edges of it, as if it were viewed through a prism. To correct this inconvenience had been long a desideratum in the art. At last it came into the mind of a sagacious optician to inquire how this matter was managed in the eye, in which there was exactly the same difficulty to contend with as in the telescope. His observation taught him that in the eye the evil was cured by combining lenses composed of different substances, that is, of substances which possessed different refracting powers. Our artist borrowed thence his hint and produced a correction of the defect by imitating, in glasses made from different materials, the effects of the different humors through which the rays of light pass before they reach the bottom of the eye. Could this be in the eye without purpose, which suggested to the optician the only effectual means of attaining that purpose?

But further, there are other points not so much perhaps of strict resemblance between the two as of superiority of the eye over the telescope, yet of a superiority which, being founded in the laws that regulate both, may furnish topics of fair and just comparison. Two things were wanted to the eye, which were not wanted, at least in the same degree, to the telescope; and these were the adaptation of the organ, first, to different degrees of light, and secondly, to the vast diversity of distance at which objects are viewed by the naked eye, namely, from a few inches to as many miles. These difficulties present not themselves to the maker of the telescope. He wants all the light he can get; and he never directs his instrument to objects near at hand. In the eye, both these cases were to be provided for; and for the purpose of providing for them, a subtle and appropriate mechanism is introduced.

.   .   .   .

Observe a newborn child first lifting up its eyelids. What does the opening of the curtain discover? The anterior part of two pellucid globes, which, when they come to be examined, are found to be constructed upon strict optical principles—the selfsame principles upon which we ourselves construct optical instruments. We find them perfect for the purpose of forming an image by refraction, composed of parts executing different offices, one part having fulfilled its office upon the pencil of light, delivering it over to the action of another part, that to a third, and so onward: the progressive action depending for its success upon the nicest and minutest adjustment of the parts concerned, yet these parts so in fact adjusted as to produce, not by a simple action or effect but by a combination of actions and effects, the result which is ultimately wanted. And forasmuch as this organ would have to operate under different circumstances with strong degrees of light and with weak degrees upon near objects and upon remote ones, and these differences demanded, according to the laws by which the transmission of light is regulated, a corresponding diversity of structure—that the aperture, for example, through which the light passes should be larger or less, the lenses rounder or flatter, or that their distance from the tablet upon which the picture is delineated should be shortened or lengthened—this, I say, being the case, and the difficulty to which the eye was to be adapted, we find its several parts capable of being occasionally changed, and a most artificial apparatus provided to produce that change. This is far beyond the common regulator of a watch, which requires the touch of a foreign hand to set it; but it is not altogether unlike Harrison's contrivance for making a watch regulate itself, by inserting within it a machinery which, by the artful use of the different expansion of metals, preserves the equability of the motion under all the various temperatures of heat and cold in which the instrument may happen to be placed.[1] The ingenuity of this last contrivance has been justly praised. Shall, therefore, a structure which differs from it chiefly by surpassing it be accounted no contrivance at all; or, if it be a contrivance, that it is without a contriver?

.   .   .   .

One question may possibly have dwelt in the reader's mind during the perusal of these observations, namely, why should not the Deity have given to the animal the faculty of vision *at once?* Why this circuitous perception; the ministry of so many means; an element provided for the purpose; reflected from opaque substances, refracted through transparent ones, and both according to precise laws; then a complex organ, an intricate and artificial apparatus, in order, by the operation of this element and in conformity with the restrictions of these laws, to produce an image upon a membrane communicating

---

[1] [John Harrison (1693-1776) was an English inventor and mechanic who in 1726 devised a "gridiron pendulum" so composed of steel and brass that changes due to expansion and contraction were exactly compensated for.]

with the brain? Wherefore all this? Why make the difficulty in order to surmount it? If to perceive objects by some other mode than that of touch, or objects which lay out of the reach of that sense, were the thing proposed, could not a simple volition of the Creator have communicated the capacity? Why resort to contrivance where power is omnipotent? Contrivance, by its very definition and nature, is the refuge of imperfection. To have recourse to expedients implies difficulty, impediment, restraint, defect of power. This question belongs to the other senses as well as to sight; to the general functions of animal life, as nutrition, secretion, respiration; to the economy of vegetables—and indeed to almost all the operations of nature. The question, therefore, is of very wide extent; and among other answers which may be given to it, beside reasons of which probably we are ignorant, one answer is this: it is only by the display of contrivance that the existence, the agency, the wisdom of the Deity *could* be testified to his rational creatures. This is the scale by which we ascend to all the knowledge of our Creator which we possess, so far as it depends upon the phenomena or the works of nature. Take away this, and you take away from us every subject of observation and ground of reasoning; I mean, as our rational faculties are formed at present. Whatever is done, God could have done without the intervention of instruments or means; but it is in the construction of instruments, in the choice and adaptation of means, that a creative intelligence is seen. It is this which constitutes the order and beauty of the universe. God, therefore, has been pleased to prescribe limits to his own power and to work his ends within those limits. The general laws of matter have perhaps prescribed the nature of these limits; its inertia; its reaction; the laws which govern the communication of motion, the refraction and reflection of light, and the constitution of fluids nonelastic and elastic, the transmission of sound through the latter; the laws of magnetism, of electricity, and probably others yet undiscovered. These are general laws; and when a particular purpose is to be effected, it is not by making a new law, nor by the suspension of the old ones, nor by making them wind and bend, and yield to the occasion—for nature with great steadiness adheres to and supports them—but it is, as we have seen in the eye, by the interposition of an apparatus corresponding with these laws, and suited to the exigency which results from them, that the purpose is at length attained. As we have said, therefore, God prescribes limits to his power that he may let in the exercise and thereby exhibit demonstrations of his wisdom. For then—that is, such laws and limitations being laid down—it is as though one Being should have fixed certain rules, and, if we may so speak, provided certain materials, and afterwards have committed to another Being, out of these materials and in subordination to these rules, the task of drawing forth a creation: a supposition which evidently leaves room and induces indeed a necessity for contrivance. Nay, there may be many such agents, and many ranks of these. We do not advance this as a doctrine either of philosophy or of religion; but we say that the subject may safely be represented under this view, because the Deity, acting himself by general laws, will have the same consequences upon our reasoning as if he had prescribed these laws to another. It has been said that the problem of creation was "attraction and matter being given, to make a world out of them"; and, as above explained, this statement perhaps does not convey a false idea.

. . . .

CHAPTER FIVE

APPLICATION OF THE ARGUMENT
CONTINUED

Every observation which was made in our first chapter concerning the watch may be repeated with strict propriety concerning the eye, concerning animals, concerning plants, concerning, indeed, all the organized parts of the works of nature. As,

I. When we are inquiring simply after the *existence* of an intelligent Creator, imperfection, inaccuracy, liability to disorder, occasional irregularities may subsist in a considerable degree without inducing any doubt into the question; just as a watch may frequently go wrong, seldom perhaps exactly right, may be faulty in some parts, defective in some, without the smallest ground of suspicion from thence arising that it was not a watch, not made, or not made for the purpose ascribed to it. When faults are pointed out, and when a question is started concerning the skill of the artist or the dexterity with which the work is executed, then, indeed, in order to defend these qualities from accusation, we must be able either to expose some intractableness and imperfection in the materials or point out some invincible difficulty in the execution, into which imperfection and difficulty the matter of complaint may be resolved; or, if we cannot do this, we must adduce such specimens of consummate art and contrivance proceeding from the same hand as may convince the inquirer of the existence, in the case before him, of impediments like those which we have mentioned, although, what from the nature of the case is very likely to happen, they be unknown and unperceived by him. This we must do in order to vindicate the artist's skill, or at least the perfection of it; as we must also judge of his intention and of the provisions employed in fulfilling that intention, not from an instance in which they fail but from the great plurality of instances in which they succeed. But, after all, these are different questions from the question of the artist's existence; or, which is the same, whether the thing before us be a work of art or not; and the questions ought always to be kept separate in the mind. So likewise it is in the works of nature. Irregularities and imperfections are of little or no weight in the consideration when that consideration relates simply to the existence of a Creator. When the argument respects his attributes, they are of weight; but are then to be taken in conjunction—the attention is not to rest upon them, but they are to be taken in conjunction with the unexceptional evidences which we possess of skill, power, and benevolence displayed in other instances; which evidences may, in strength, number, and variety, be such and may so overpower apparent blemishes as to induce us, upon the most reasonable ground, to believe that these last ought to be referred to some cause, though we be ignorant of it, other than defect of knowledge or of benevolence in the author.

II. There may be also parts of plants and animals, as there were supposed to be of the watch, of which in some instances the operation, in others the use, is unknown. These form different cases; for the operation may be unknown, yet the use be certain. Thus it is with the lungs of animals. It does not, I think, appear that we are acquainted with the action of the air upon the blood, or in what manner that action is communicated by the lungs; yet we find that a very short suspension of their office destroys the life of the animal. In this case, therefore, we may be said to know the use, nay, we experience the necessity of the organ though we be ignorant of its operation. Nearly the same thing may be observed of what is called the lymphatic system. We suffer grievous inconveniences from its disorder, without being informed of the office which it sustains in the economy of our bodies. There may possibly also be some few examples of the second class in which not only the operation is unknown, but in which experiments may seem to prove that the part is not necessary;

or may leave a doubt how far it is even useful to the plant or animal in which it is found. This is said to be the case with the spleen, which has been extracted from dogs without any sensible injury to their vital functions. Instances of the former kind, namely, in which we cannot explain the operation, may be numerous; for they will be so in proportion to our ignorance. They will be more or fewer to different persons, and in different stages of science. Every improvement of knowledge diminishes their number. There is hardly, perhaps, a year passes that does not in the works of nature bring some operation or some mode of operation to light, which was before undiscovered—probably unsuspected. Instances of the second kind, namely, where the part appears to be totally useless, I believe to be extremely rare; compared with the number of those of which the use is evident, they are beneath any assignable proportion and perhaps have been never submitted to trial and examination sufficiently accurate, long enough continued, or often enough repeated. No accounts which I have seen are satisfactory. The mutilated animal may live and grow fat—as was the case of the dog deprived of its spleen—yet may be defective in some other of its functions, which, whether they can all, or in what degree of vigor and perfection, be performed, or how long preserved without the extirpated organ, does not seem to be ascertained by experiment. But to this case, even were it fully made out, may be applied the consideration which we suggested concerning the watch, namely, that these superfluous parts do not negative the reasoning which we instituted concerning those parts which are useful, and of which we know the use; the indication of contrivance with respect to them remains as it was before.

III. One atheistic way of replying to our observations upon the works of nature, and to the proofs of a Deity which we think that we perceive in them, is to tell us that all which we see must necessarily have had some form, and that it might as well be its present form as any other. Let us now apply this answer to the eye, as we did before to the watch. Something or other must have occupied that place in the animal's head, must have filled up, as we say, that socket; we will say, also, that it must have been of that sort of substance which we call animal substance, as flesh, bone, membrane, or cartilage, etc. But that it should have been an *eye*, knowing as we do what an eye comprehends, namely, that it should have consisted, first, of a series of transparent lenses—very different, by the by, even in their substance, from the opaque materials of which the rest of the body is, in general at least, composed, and with which the whole of its surface, this single portion of it excepted, is covered; secondly, of a black cloth or canvas— the only membrane in the body which is black—spread out behind these lenses, so as to receive the image formed by pencils of light transmitted through them, and at which alone a distinct image could be formed, namely, at the concourse of the refracted rays; thirdly, of a large nerve communicating between this membrane and the brain, without which the action of light upon the membrane, however modified by the organ, would be lost to the purposes of sensation; that this fortunate conformation of parts should have been the lot not of one individual out of many thousand individuals, like the great prize in a lottery or like some singularity in nature, but the happy chance of a whole species; nor of one species out of many thousand species with which we are acquainted, but of by far the greatest number of all that exist, and that under varieties not casual or capricious, but bearing marks of being suited to their respective exigencies; that all this should have taken place merely because something must have occupied these points on every animal's forehead, or that all this should be thought to be accounted for by the short answer that "whatever was there must have had some form or other" is too absurd to be made more so by any argumentation. We are not contented with this answer; we find no satisfaction in it, by way of accounting for appearances of organization far short of those of the eye, such as we observe in fossil shells, petrified bones, or other substances which bear the vestiges of animal or vegetable recrements, but which, either in respect to utility or of the situation in which they are discovered, may seem accidental enough. It is no way of accounting even for these things, to say that the stone, for instance, which is shown to us—supposing the question to be concerning a petrifaction—must have contained some internal conformation or other. Nor does it mend the answer to add, with respect to the singularity of the conformation, that after the event it is no longer to be computed what the chances were against it. This is always to be computed when the question is whether a useful or imitative conformation be the product of chance or not: I desire no greater certainty in reasoning than that by which chance is excluded from the present disposition of the natural world. Universal experience is against it. What does chance ever do for us? In the human body, for instance, chance, that is, the operation of causes without design, may produce a wen, a wart, a mole, a pimple, but never an eye. Among inanimate substances, a clod, a pebble, a liquid drop might be; but never was a watch, a telescope, an organized body of any kind, answering a valuable purpose by a complicated mechanism, the effect of chance. In no assignable instance has such a thing existed without intention somewhere.

IV. There is another answer which has the same effect as the resolving of things into chance, which answer would persuade us to believe that the eye, the animal to which it belongs, every other animal, every plant, indeed every organized body which we see are only so many out of the possible varieties and combinations of being which the lapse of infinite ages has brought into existence; that the present world is the relic of that variety; millions of other bodily forms and other species having perished, being, by the defect of their constitution, incapable of preservation, or of continuance by generation. Now there is no foundation whatever for this conjecture in any thing which we observe in the works of nature; no such experiments are going on at present—no such energy operates as that which is here supposed, and which should be constantly pushing into existence new varieties of beings. Nor are there any appearances to support an opinion that every possible combination of vegetable or animal structure has formerly been tried. Multitudes of conformation, both of vegetables and animals, may be conceived capable of existence and succession, which yet do not exist. Perhaps almost as many forms of plants might have been found in the fields as figures of plants can be delineated upon paper. A countless variety of animals might have existed which do not exist. Upon the supposition here stated, we should see unicorns and mermaids, sylphs and centaurs, the fancies of painters and the fables of poets, realized by examples. Or, if it be alleged that these may transgress the bounds of possible life and propagation, we might at least have nations of human beings without nails upon their fingers, with more or fewer fingers and toes than ten, some with one eye, others with one ear, with one nostril, or without the sense of smelling at all. All these and a thousand other imaginable varieties might live and propagate. We may modify any one species many different ways, all consistent with life, and with the actions necessary to preservation, although affording different degrees of conveniency and enjoyment to the animal. And if we carry these modifications through the different species which are known to subsist, their number would be incalculable. No reason can be given why, if these deperdits [2] ever existed, they have now disappeared. Yet, if all possible existences have been tried, they must have formed part of the catalogue.

But, moreover, the division of organized substances into animals and vegetables, and the distribution and subdistribution of each into genera and species, which distribution is not an arbitrary act of the mind, but founded in the order which prevails in external nature, appear to me to contradict the supposition of the present world being the remains of an indefinite variety of existences—of a variety which rejects all plan. The hypothesis teaches that every possible variety of being has at one time or other found its way into existence—by what cause or in what manner is not said—and that those which were badly formed perished; but how or why those which survived should be cast, as we see that plants and ani-

[2] [Lost species.]

mals are cast, into regular classes, the hypothesis does not explain; or rather the hypothesis is inconsistent with this phenomenon.

The hypothesis, indeed, is hardly deserving of the consideration which we have given it. What should we think of a man who, because we had never ourselves seen watches, telescopes, stocking mills, steam engines, etc., made, knew not how they were made, nor could prove by testimony when they were made, or by whom, would have us believe that these machines, instead of deriving their curious structures from the thought and design of their inventors and contrivers, in truth derive them from no other origin than this: namely, that a mass of metals and other materials having run, when melted, into all possible figures, and combined themselves in all possible forms and shapes and proportions, these things which we see are what were left from the incident, as best worth preserving, and as such are become the remaining stock of a magazine which, at one time or other, has by this means contained every mechanism, useful and useless, convenient and inconvenient, into which such like materials could be thrown? I cannot distinguish the hypothesis, as applied to the works of nature, from this solution, which no one would accept as applied to a collection of machines.

V. To the marks of contrivance discoverable in animal bodies, and to the argument deduced from them in proof of design and of a designing Creator, this turn is sometimes attempted to be given, namely, that the parts were not intended for the use, but that the use arose out of the parts. This distinction is intelligible. A cabinetmaker rubs his mahogany with fish skin; yet it would be too much to assert that the skin of the dogfish was made rough and granulated on purpose for the polishing of wood, and the use of cabinetmakers. Therefore the distinction is intelligible. But I think that there is very little place for it in the works of nature. When roundly and generally affirmed of them, as it has sometimes been, it amounts to such another stretch of assertion as it would be to say that all the implements of the cabinetmaker's workshop,

as well as his fish skin, were substances accidentally config-
urated, which he had picked up and converted to his use; that
his adzes, saws, planes, and gimlets were not made, as we suppose, to hew, cut, smooth, shape out, or bore wood with, but
that, these things being made, no matter with what design, or
whether with any, the cabinetmaker perceived that they were
applicable to his purpose and turned them to account.

But, again, so far as this solution is attempted to be applied
to those parts of animals the action of which does not depend
upon the will of the animal, it is fraught with still more evident absurdity. Is it possible to believe that the eye was
formed without any regard to vision; that it was the animal
itself which found out that, though formed with no such intention, it would serve to see with; and that the use of the eye
as an organ of sight resulted from this discovery, and the animal's application of it? The same question may be asked of
the ear; the same of all the senses. None of the senses funda-
mentally depend upon the election of the animal; consequently neither upon his sagacity nor his experience. It is
the impression which objects make upon them that constitutes
their use. Under that impression he is passive. He may bring
objects to the sense, or within its reach; he may select these objects; but over the impression itself he has no power, or very
little; and that properly is the sense.

Secondly, there are many parts of animal bodies which seem
to depend upon the will of the animal in a greater degree than
the senses do, and yet with respect to which this solution is
equally unsatisfactory. If we apply the solution to the human
body, for instance, it forms itself into questions upon which
no reasonable mind can doubt: such as, whether the teeth
were made expressly for the mastication of food, the feet for
walking, the hands for holding; or whether, these things as
they are being in fact in the animal's possession, his own ingenuity taught him that they were convertible to these purposes, though no such purposes were contemplated in their
formation.

All that there is of the appearance of reason in this way

of considering the subject is that, in some cases, the organization seems to determine the habits of the animal and its choice to a particular mode of life which in a certain sense may be called "the use arising out of the part." Now, to all the instances in which there is any place for this suggestion, it may be replied that the organization determines the animal to habits beneficial and salutary to itself, and that this effect would not be seen so regularly to follow, if the several organizations did not bear a concerted and contrived relation to the substance by which the animal was surrounded. They would, otherwise, be capacities without objects—powers without employment. The webfoot determines, you say, the duck to swim; but what would that avail if there were no water to swim in? The strong hooked bill and sharp talons of one species of bird determine it to prey upon animals; the soft straight bill and weak claws of another species determine it to pick up seeds; but neither determination could take effect in providing for the sustenance of the birds, if animal bodies and vegetable seeds did not lie within their reach. The peculiar conformation of the bill and tongue and claws of the woodpecker determines that bird to search for his food among the insects lodged behind the bark or in the wood of decayed trees; but what would this profit him if there were no trees, no decayed trees, no insects lodged under their bark or in their trunk? The proboscis with which the bee is furnished determines him to seek for honey; but what would that signify if flowers supplied none? Faculties thrown down upon animals at random, and without reference to the objects amidst which they are placed, would not produce to them the services and benefits which we see; and if there be that reference, then there is intention.

Lastly, the solution fails entirely when applied to plants. The parts of plants answer their uses without any concurrence from the will or choice of the plant.

VI. Others have chosen to refer every thing to a *principle of order* in nature. A principle of order is the word; but what is meant by a principle of order as different from an intelligent

Creator has not been explained either by definition or example; and without such explanation it should seem to be a mere substitution of words for reasons, names for causes. Order itself is only the adaptation of means to an end: a principle of order, therefore, can only signify the mind and intention which so adapts them. Or, were it capable of being explained in any other sense, is there any experience, any analogy, to sustain it? Was a watch ever produced by a principle of order; and why might not a watch be so produced as well as an eye?

Furthermore, a principle of order, acting blindly and without choice, is negatived by the observation that order is not universal, which it would be if it issued from a constant and necessary principle, nor indiscriminate, which it would be if it issued from an unintelligent principle. Where order is wanted, there we find it; where order is not wanted, that is, where if it prevailed, it would be useless, there we do not find it. In the structure of the eye—for we adhere to our example—in the figure and position of its several parts, the most exact order is maintained. In the forms of rocks and mountains, in the lines which bound the coasts of continents and islands, in the shape of bays and promontories, no order whatever is perceived, because it would have been superfluous. No useful purpose would have arisen from molding rocks and mountains into regular solids, bounding the channel of the ocean by geometrical curves, or from the map of the world resembling a table of diagrams in Euclid's *Elements* or Simpson's "Conic Sections." [3]

VII. Lastly, the confidence which we place in our observations upon the works of nature, in the marks which we discover of contrivance, choice, and design, and in our reasoning upon the proofs afforded us, ought not to be shaken, as it is sometimes attempted to be done, by bringing forward to our view our own ignorance, or rather the general imperfection of

---

[3] [Thomas Simpson (1710-61), English mathematician. Paley was probably referring here to a portion of Simpson's *Essays on Several Curious and Useful Subjects in Speculative and Mixed Mathematics* (London, 1740).]

our knowledge of nature. Nor, in many cases, ought this consideration to affect us even when it respects some parts of the subject immediately under our notice. True fortitude of understanding consists in not suffering what we know, to be disturbed by what we do not know. If we perceive a useful end, and means adapted to that end, we perceive enough for our conclusion. If these things be clear, no matter what is obscure. The argument is finished. For instance, if the utility of vision to the animal which enjoys it, and the adaptation of the *eye* to this office, be evident and certain—and I can mention nothing which is more so—ought it to prejudice the inference which we draw from these premises, that we cannot explain the use of the spleen? Nay, more, if there be parts of the eye, namely, the cornea, the crystalline, the retina, in their substance, figure and position, manifestly suited to the formation of an image by the refraction of rays of light, at least as manifestly as the glasses and tubes of a dioptric telescope are suited to that purpose, it concerns not the proof which these afford of design, and of a designer, that there may perhaps be other parts, certain muscles, for instance, or nerves in the same eye, of the agency or effect of which we can give no account, any more than we should be inclined to doubt, or ought to doubt, about the construction of a telescope, namely, for what purpose it was constructed, or whether it was constructed at all, because there belonged to it certain screws and pins, the use or action of which we did not comprehend. I take it to be a general way of infusing doubts and scruples into the mind, to recur to its own ignorance, its own imbecility—to tell us that upon these subjects we know little; that little imperfectly; or rather, that we know nothing properly about the matter. These suggestions so fall in with our consciousness as sometimes to produce a general distrust of our faculties and our conclusions. But this is an unfounded jealousy. The uncertainty of one thing does not necessarily affect the certainty of another thing. Our ignorance of many points need not suspend our assurance of a few. Before we yield, in any particular instance, to the skepticism which this sort of insinuation would induce, we ought accurately to ascertain whether our ignorance or doubt concern those precise points upon which our conclusion rests. Other points are nothing. Our ignorance of other points may be of no consequence to these, though they be points, in various respects, of great importance. A just reasoner removes from his consideration not only what he knows, but what he does not know, touching matters not strictly connected with his argument, that is, not forming the very steps of his deduction: beyond these, his knowledge and his ignorance are alike relative.

CHAPTER SIX

THE ARGUMENT CUMULATIVE

Were there no example in the world of contrivance except that of the *eye,* it would be alone sufficient to support the conclusion which we draw from it, as to the necessity of an intelligent Creator. It could never be got rid of, because it could not be accounted for by any other supposition which did not contradict all the principles we possess of knowledge—the principles according to which things do, as often as they can be brought to the test of experience, turn out to be true or false. Its coats and humors, constructed as the lenses of a telescope are constructed, for the refraction of rays of light to a point, which forms the proper action of the organ; the provision in its muscular tendons for turning its pupil to the object, similar to that which is given to the telescope by screws, and upon which power of direction in the eye the exercise of its office as an optical instrument depends; the further provision for its defense, for its constant lubricity and moisture, which we see in its socket and its lids, in its glands for the secretion of the matter of tears, its outlet or communication with the nose for carrying off the liquid after the eye is washed with it; these provisions compose altogether an apparatus, a system of parts, a preparation of means, so manifest in their design, so exquisite in their contrivance, so successful in their issue, so precious, and so infinitely beneficial in their use, as, in my opinion, to bear down all doubt that can be raised upon the subject. And what I wish, under the title of the present chapter, to observe is that, if other parts of nature were inaccessible to our inquiries, or even if other parts of nature presented nothing to our examination but disorder and confusion, the validity of this example would remain the same. If there were but one watch in the world, it would not be less certain that it had a maker. If we had never in our lives seen any but one single kind of hydraulic machine, yet if of that one kind we understood the mechanism and use, we should be as perfectly assured that it proceeded from the hand and thought and skill of a workman, as if we visited a museum of the arts and saw collected there twenty different kinds of machines for drawing water, or a thousand different kinds for other purposes. Of this point each machine is a proof independently of all the rest. So it is with the evidences of a divine agency. The proof is not a conclusion which lies at the end of a chain of reasoning, of which chain each instance of contrivance is only a link, and of which, if one link fail, the whole fails; but it is an argument separately supplied by every separate example. An error in stating an example affects only that example. The argument is cumulative in the fullest sense of that term. The eye proves it without the ear; the ear without the eye. The proof in each example is complete; for when the design of the part and the conduciveness of its structure to that design is shown, the mind may set itself at rest; no future consideration can detract anything from the force of the example.

CHAPTER TWENTY-THREE

OF THE PERSONALITY OF THE DEITY

Contrivance, if established, appears to me to prove everything which we wish to prove. Among other things, it proves the *personality* of the Deity, as distinguished from what is sometimes called nature, sometimes called a principle; which terms, in the mouths of those who use them philosophically, seem to be intended to admit and to express an efficacy, but to exclude and to deny a personal agent. Now, that which can contrive, which can design, must be a person. These capacities constitute personality, for they imply consciousness and thought. They require that which can perceive an end or purpose, as well as the power of providing means and directing them to their end.[4] They require a center in which perceptions unite, and from which volitions flow; which is mind. The acts of a mind prove the existence of a mind; and in whatever a mind resides, is a person. The seat of intellect is a person. We have no authority to limit the properties of mind to any particular corporeal form or to any particular circumscription of space. These properties subsist in created nature under a great variety of sensible forms. Also, every animated being has its *sensorium*, that is, a certain portion of space within which perception and volition are exerted. This sphere may be enlarged to an indefinite extent—may comprehend the universe; and being so imagined, may serve to furnish us with as good

4 [Joseph] Priestley, *Letters to a Philosophical Unbeliever*, 2nd edn. [(Birmingham and London, 1787), Part I,] p. 253 [misprinted as p. 153].
[Joseph Priestley (1733-1804), English scientist and liberal theologian, best known for his discovery of oxygen, published Part I of his *Letters to a Philosophical Unbeliever* in 1780. The *Letters* were written against Hume and were supplemented with additional remarks published in 1782.]

a notion as we are capable of forming, of the *immensity* of the divine nature, that is, of a Being, infinite, as well in essence as in power, yet nevertheless a person.

"No man hath seen God at any time." [5] And this, I believe, makes the great difficulty. Now, it is a difficulty which chiefly arises from our not duly estimating the state of our faculties. The Deity, it is true, is the object of none of our senses; but reflect what limited capacities animal senses are. Many animals seem to have but one sense, or perhaps two at the most —touch and taste. Ought such an animal to conclude against the existence of odors, sounds, and colors? To another species is given the sense of smelling. This is an advance in the knowledge of the powers and properties of nature; but if this favored animal should infer from its superiority over the class last described, that it perceived everything which was perceptible in nature, it is known to us, though perhaps not suspected by the animal itself, that it proceeded upon a false and presumptuous estimate of its faculties. To another is added the sense of hearing; which lets in a class of sensations entirely unconceived by the animal before spoken of, not only distinct, but remote from any which *it* had ever experienced, and greatly superior to them. Yet this last animal has no more ground for believing that its senses comprehend all things and all properties of things which exist, than might have been claimed by the tribes of animals beneath it; for we know that it is still possible to possess another sense, that of sight, which shall disclose to the percipient a new world. This fifth sense makes the animal what the human animal is; but to infer that possibility stops here, that either this fifth sense is the last sense, or that the five comprehend all existence, is just as unwarrantable a conclusion as that which might have been made by any of the different species which possessed only one. The conclusion of the one-sense animal and the conclusion of the five-sense animal stand upon the same authority. There may be more and other senses than those which we have. There may be senses suited to the perception of the powers, properties, and

5 [John 1:18.]

substance of spirits. These may belong to higher orders of rational agents; for there is not the smallest reason for supposing that we are the highest, or that the scale of creation stops with us.

The great *energies* of nature are known to us only by their effects. The substances which produce them are as much concealed from our senses as the divine essence itself. *Gravitation,* though constantly present, though constantly exerting its influence, though everywhere around us, near us, and within us —though diffused throughout all space, and penetrating the texture of all bodies with which we are acquainted, depends, if upon a fluid, upon a fluid which, though both powerful and universal in its operation, is no object of sense to us; if upon any other kind of substance or action, upon a substance and action from which *we* receive no distinguishable impressions. Is it then to be wondered at that it should in some measure be the same with the divine nature?

Of this, however, we are certain, that whatever the Deity be, neither the *universe,* nor any part of it which we see, can be he. The universe itself is merely a collective name; its parts are all which are real, or which are *things.* Now inert matter is out of the question; and organized substances include marks of contrivance. But whatever includes marks of contrivance, whatever in its constitution testifies design, necessarily carries us to something beyond itself, to some other being, to a designer prior to and out of itself. No animal, for instance, can have contrived its own limbs and senses—can have been the author to itself of the design with which they were constructed. That supposition involves all the absurdity of self-creation, that is, of acting without existing. Nothing can be God which is ordered by a wisdom and a will which itself is void of— which is indebted for any of its properties to contrivance *ab extra.* The *not* having that in his nature which requires the exertion of another prior being—which property is sometimes called self-sufficiency, and sometimes self-comprehension—appertains to the Deity, as his essential distinction, and removes his nature from that of all things which we see: which consideration contains the answer to a question that has sometimes been asked, namely, why, since some other thing must have existed from eternity, may not the present universe be that something? The contrivance perceived in it proves that to be impossible. Nothing contrived can, in a strict and proper sense, be eternal, forasmuch as the contriver must have existed before the contrivance.

Wherever we see marks of contrivance, we are led for its cause to an *intelligent* author. And this transition of the understanding is founded upon uniform experience. We see intelligence constantly contriving; that is, we see intelligence constantly producing effects, marked and distinguished by certain properties—not certain particular properties, but by a kind and class of properties, such as relation to an end, relation of parts to one another and to a common purpose. We see, wherever we are witnesses to the actual formation of things, nothing except intelligence producing effects so marked and distinguished in the same manner. We wish to account for their origin. Our experience suggests a cause perfectly adequate to this account. No experience, no single instance or example, can be offered in favor of any other. In this cause, therefore, we ought to rest; in this cause the common sense of mankind has, in fact, rested, because it agrees with that which in all cases is the foundation of knowledge—the undeviating course of their experience. The reasoning is the same as that by which we conclude any ancient appearances to have been the effects of volcanoes or inundations, namely, because they resemble the effects which fire and water produce before our eyes, and because we have never known these effects to result from any other operation. And this resemblance may subsist in so many circumstances as not to leave us under the smallest doubt in forming our opinion. Men are not deceived by this reasoning; for whenever it happens, as it sometimes does happen, that the truth comes to be known by direct information, it turns out to be what was expected. In like manner and upon the same foundation—which in truth is that of experience—we conclude that the works of nature proceed from intelligence and design; because, in the properties of relation to a purpose, subserviency to a use, they resemble what intelligence and design are constantly producing, and what nothing except intelligence and design ever produce at all. Of every argument which would raise a question as to the safety of this reasoning, it may be observed that if such argument be listened to, it leads to the inference not only that the present order of nature is insufficient to prove the existence of an intelligent Creator, but that no imaginable order would be sufficient to prove it —that *no* contrivance, were it ever so mechanical, ever so precise, ever so clear, ever so perfectly like those which we ourselves employ, would support this conclusion: a doctrine to which I conceive no sound mind can assent.

The force, however, of the reasoning is sometimes sunk by our taking up with mere names. We have already noticed,[6] and we must here notice again, the misapplication of the term "law," and the mistake concerning the idea which that term expresses in physics, whenever such idea is made to take the place of power, and still more of an intelligent power, and, as such, to be assigned for the cause of any thing, or of any property of any thing that exists. This is what we are secretly apt to do, when we speak of organized bodies—plants, for instance, or animals—owning their production, their form, their growth, their qualities, their beauty, their use, to any law or laws of nature; and when we are contented to sit down with that answer to our inquiries concerning them. I say once more, that it is a perversion of language to assign any law as the efficient, operative cause of any thing. A law presupposes an agent, for it is only the mode according to which an agent proceeds; it implies a power, for it is the order according to which that power acts. Without this agent, without this power, which are both distinct from itself, the "law" does nothing, is nothing.

What has been said concerning "law" holds true of *mechanism*. Mechanism is not itself power. Mechanism without power can do nothing. Let a watch be contrived and con-

6 Chapter One, Section VII [p. 6].

structed ever so ingeniously—be its parts ever so many, ever
so complicated, ever so finely wrought or artificially put together, it cannot *go* without a weight or spring; that is, without a force independent of, and ulterior to its mechanism.
The spring, acting at the center, will produce different motions and different results, according to the variety of the intermediate mechanism. One and the selfsame spring, acting in
one and the same manner, namely, by simply expanding itself,
may be the cause of a hundred different and all useful movements, if a hundred different and well-devised sets of wheels
be placed between it and the final effect: for example, [it] may
point out the hour of the day, the day of the month, the age
of the moon, the position of the planets, the cycle of the years,
and many other serviceable notices; and these movements may
fulfill their purposes with more or less perfection, according
as the mechanism is better or worse contrived, or better or
worse executed, or in a better or worse state of repair; *but in
all cases it is necessary that the spring act at the center.* The
course of our reasoning upon such a subject would be this:
by inspecting the watch, even when standing still, we get a
proof of contrivance, and of a contriving mind having been
employed about it. In the form and obvious relation of its
parts, we see enough to convince us of this. If we pull the
works in pieces, for the purpose of a closer examination, we
are still more fully convinced. But when we see the watch
going, we see proof of another point, namely, that there is a
power somewhere, and somehow or other applied to it—a
power in action; that there is more in the subject than the
mere wheels of the machine; that there is a secret spring, or
a gravitating plummet; in a word, that there is force and energy as well as mechanism.

So then, the watch in motion establishes to the observer
two conclusions: one, that thought, contrivance, and design
have been employed in the forming, proportioning, and arranging of its parts, and that whoever or wherever he be, or
were, such a contriver there is, or was; the other, that force or
power, distinct from mechanism, is at this present time acting

upon it. If I saw it grinding, I should be assured that a hand was at the windlass, though in another room. It is the same in nature. In the works of nature we trace mechanism, and this alone proves contrivance; but living, active, moving, productive nature proves also the exertion of a power at the center; for wherever the power resides may be denominated the center.

The intervention and disposition of what are called *second causes* fall under the same observation. This disposition is or is not mechanism, according as we can or cannot trace it by our senses and means of examination. That is all the difference there is; and it is a difference which respects our faculties, not the things themselves. Now, where the order of second causes is mechanical, what is here said of mechanism strictly applies to it. But it would be always mechanism—natural chemistry, for instance, would be mechanism—if our senses were acute enough to descry it. Neither mechanism, therefore, in the works of nature, nor the intervention of what are called second causes—for I think that they are the same thing—excuses the necessity of an agent distinct from both.

If, in tracing these causes, it be said that we find certain general properties of matter which have nothing in them that bespeaks intelligence, I answer that still the *managing* of these properties, the pointing and directing them to the uses which we see made of them, demands intelligence in the highest degree. For example, suppose animal secretions to be elective attractions, and that such and such attractions universally belong to such and such substances—in all which there is no intellect concerned; still, the choice and collocation of these substances, the fixing upon right substances, and disposing them in right places must be an act of intelligence. What mischief would follow were there a single transposition of the secretory organs; a single mistake in arranging the glands which compose them!

There may be many second causes, and many courses of second causes, one behind another, between what we observe of nature and the Deity, but there must be intelligence somewhere—there must be more in nature than what we see; and,

among the things unseen, there must be an intelligent, designing author. The philosopher beholds with astonishment the
production of things around him. Unconscious particles of
matter take their stations, and severally range themselves in
an order, so as to become collectively plants or animals, that
is, organized bodies, with parts bearing strict and evident
relation to one another and to the utility of the whole; and
it should seem that these particles could not move in any
other way than as they do, for they testify not the smallest
sign of choice, or liberty, or discretion. There may be particular intelligent beings guiding these motions in each case;
or they may be the result of trains of mechanical dispositions,
fixed beforehand by an intelligent appointment and kept in
action by a power at the center. But, in either case, there must
be intelligence.

The minds of most men are fond of what they call a
principle, and of the appearance of simplicity, in accounting
for phenomena. Yet this principle, this simplicity, resides
merely in the *name;* which name, after all, comprises perhaps under it a diversified, multifarious, or progressive operation, distinguishable into parts. The power in organized
bodies of producing bodies like themselves is one of these
principles. Give a philosopher this and he can get on. But
he does not reflect what this mode of production, this principle—if such he choose to call it—requires; how much it presupposes; what an apparatus of instruments, some of which
are strictly mechanical, is necessary to its success; what a train
it includes of operations and changes, one succeeding another,
one related to another, one ministering to another; all advancing by intermediate, and frequently by sensible steps, to their
ultimate result. Yet, because the whole of this complicated
action is wrapped up in a single term, *generation,* we are to
set it down as an elementary principle and to suppose that
when we have resolved the things which we see into this
principle, we have sufficiently accounted for their origin without the necessity of a designing, intelligent Creator. The truth
is, generation is not a principle, but a *process.* We might as

well call the casting of metals a principle; we might, so far
as appears to me, as well call spinning and weaving principles;
and then, referring the texture of cloths, the fabric of muslins
and calicoes, the patterns of diapers and damasks, to these, as
principles, pretend to dispense with intention, thought, and
contrivance on the part of the artist; or to dispense, indeed,
with the necessity of any artist at all either in the manufactur-
ing of the article or in the fabrication of the machinery by
which the manufacture was carried on.

And after all, how, or in what sense is it true, that animals
produce their *like?* A butterfly with a proboscis instead of a
mouth, with four wings, and six legs, produces a hairy caterpillar with jaws and teeth, and fourteen feet. A frog produces
a tadpole. A black beetle with gauze wings and a crusty cover-
ing produces a white, smooth, soft worm; an ephemeron fly,
a cod-bait maggot. These by a progress through different
stages of life and action and enjoyment—and, in each state
provided with implements and organs appropriated to the
temporary nature which they bear—arrive at last at the form
and fashion of the parent animal. But all this is process, not
principle, and proves, moreover, that the property of animated
bodies of producing their like belongs to them, not as a
primordial property, not by any blind necessity in the nature
of things, but as the effect of economy, wisdom, and design;
because the property itself assumes diversities, and submits to
deviations dictated by intelligible utilities, and serving distinct
purposes of animal happiness.

The opinion which would consider "generation" as a *principle* in nature, and which would assign this principle as the
cause, or endeavor to satisfy our minds with such a cause of
the existence of organized bodies, is confuted, in my judgment,
not only by every mark of contrivance discoverable in those
bodies, for which it gives us no contriver, offers no account
whatever, but also by the further consideration that things
generated possess a clear relation to things *not* generated. If
it were merely one part of a generated body bearing a relation
to another part of the same body, as the mouth of an animal

to the throat, the throat to the stomach, the stomach to the intestines, those to the recruiting of the blood, and, by means of the blood, to the nourishment of the whole frame; or if it were only one generated body bearing a relation to another generated body, as the sexes of the same species to each other, animals of prey to their prey, herbivorous and granivorous animals to the plants or seeds upon which they feed, it might be contended that the whole of this correspondency was attributable to generation, the common origin from which these substances proceeded. But what shall we say to agreements which exist between things generated and things *not generated?* Can it be doubted, was it ever doubted, but that the *lungs* of animals bear a relation to the *air* as a permanently elastic fluid? They act in it and by it, they cannot act without it. Now, if generation produced the animal, it did not produce the air; yet their properties correspond. The *eye* is made for *light*, and light for the eye. The eye would be of no use without light, and light perhaps of little without eyes; yet one is produced by generation, the other not. The *ear* depends upon *undulations* of air. Here are two sets of motions: first, of the pulses of the air; secondly, of the drum, bones, and nerves of the ear—sets of motions bearing an evident reference to each other; yet the one, and the apparatus for the one, produced by the intervention of generation; the other altogether independent of it.

If it be said that the air, the light, the elements, the world itself is *generated,* I answer that I do not comprehend the proposition. If the term mean anything similar to what it means when applied to plants or animals, the proposition is certainly without proof, and I think draws as near to absurdity as any proposition can do which does not include a contradiction in its terms. I am at a loss to conceive how the formation of the world can be compared to the generation of an animal. If the term generation signify something quite different from what it signifies on ordinary occasions, it may by the same latitude signify anything. In which case, a word or phrase taken from the language of Otaheite [7] would convey

7 [Tahiti.]

as much theory concerning the origin of the universe, as it does to talk of its being generated.

We know a cause—intelligence—adequate to the appearances which we wish to account for; we have this cause continually producing similar appearances; yet, rejecting this cause, the sufficiency of which we know, and the action of which is constantly before our eyes, we are invited to resort to suppositions destitute of a single fact for their support, and confirmed by no analogy with which we are acquainted. Were it necessary to inquire into the *motives* of men's opinions, I mean their motives separate from their arguments, I should almost suspect that because the proof of a Deity drawn from the constitution of nature is not only popular, but vulgar—which may arise from the cogency of the proof and be indeed its highest recommendation—and because it is a species almost of *puerility* to take up with it; for these reasons minds which are habitually in search of invention and originality feel a resistless inclination to strike off into other solutions and other expositions. The truth is that many minds are not so indisposed to anything which can be offered to them, as they are to the *flatness* of being content with common reasons, and, what is most to be lamented, minds conscious of superiority are the most liable to this repugnancy.

. . . .

Upon the whole, after all the schemes and struggles of a reluctant philosophy, the necessary resort is to a Deity. The marks of *design* are too strong to be gotten over. Design must have had a designer. That designer must have been a person. That person is God.

CHAPTER TWENTY-FOUR

OF THE NATURAL ATTRIBUTES OF THE DEITY

It is an immense conclusion that there is a God—a perceiving, intelligent, designing Being, at the head of creation, and from whose will it proceeded. The *attributes* of such a Being, suppose his reality to be proved, must be adequate to the magnitude, extent, and multiplicity of his operations, which are not only vast beyond comparison with those performed by any other power, but so far as respects our conceptions of them, infinite, because they are unlimited on all sides.

Yet the contemplation of a nature so exalted, however surely we arrive at the proof of its existence, overwhelms our faculties. The mind feels its powers sink under the subject. One consequence of which is that from painful abstraction the thoughts seek relief in sensible images, whence may be deduced the ancient and almost universal propensity to idolatrous substitutions. They are the resources of a laboring imagination. False religions usually fall in with the natural propensity; true religions, or such as have derived themselves from the true, resist it.

It is one of the advantages of the revelations which we acknowledge, that while they reject idolatry with its many pernicious accompaniments, they introduce the Deity to human apprehension under an idea more personal, more determinate, more within its compass, than the theology of nature can do. And this they do by representing him exclusively under the relation in which he stands to ourselves; and for the most part, under some precise character, resulting from that relation or from the history of his providences; which method suits the span of our intellects much better than the universality which enters into the idea of God, as deduced from the views of nature. When, therefore, these representations are well founded in point of authority—for all depends upon that—they afford a condescension to the state of our faculties, of which they who have most reflected on the subject will be the first to acknowledge the want and the value.

Nevertheless, if we be careful to imitate the documents of our religion by confining our explanations to what concerns ourselves, and do not affect more precision in our ideas than the subject allows of, the several terms which are employed to denote the attributes of the Deity may be made, even in natural religion, to bear a sense consistent with truth and reason and not surpassing our comprehension.

These terms are omnipotence, omniscience, omnipresence, eternity, self-existence, necessary existence, spirituality.

"Omnipotence," "omniscience," "infinite" power, "infinite" knowledge are *superlatives* expressing our conception of these attributes in the strongest and most elevated terms which language supplies. We ascribe power to the Deity under the name of "omnipotence," the strict and correct conclusion being that a power which could create such a world as this is must be, beyond all comparison, greater than any which we experience in ourselves, than any which we observe in other visible agents, greater also than any which we can want, for our individual protection and preservation, in the Being upon whom we depend. It is a power likewise to which we are not authorized, by our observation or knowledge, to assign any limits of space or duration.

Very much of the same sort of remark is applicable to the term "omniscience"—infinite knowledge, or infinite wisdom. In strictness of language, there is a difference between knowledge and wisdom, wisdom always supposing action and action directed by it. With respect to the first, namely, *knowledge,* the Creator must know intimately the constitution and properties of the things which he created, which seems also to imply a foreknowledge of their action upon one another and of their changes; at least, so far as the same result from trains of physical and necessary causes. His omniscience also, as far as respects things present, is deducible from his nature, as an intelligent being, joined with the extent, or rather the universality of his operations. Where he acts, he is; and where he is, he perceives. The *wisdom* of the Deity, as testified in the works of creation, surpasses all idea we have of wisdom drawn from the highest intellectual operations of the highest class of intelligent beings with whom we are acquainted; and, which is of the chief importance to us, whatever be its compass or extent which it is evidently impossible that we should be able to determine, it must be adequate to the conduct of that order of things under which we live. And this is enough. It is of very inferior consequence by what terms we express our notion, or rather our admiration of this attribute. The terms which the piety and the usage of language have rendered habitual to us may be as proper as any other. We can trace this attribute much beyond what is necessary for any conclusion to which we have occasion to apply it. The degree of knowledge and power requisite for the formation of created nature cannot, with respect to us, be distinguished from infinite.

The divine "omnipresence" stands, in natural theology, upon this foundation: in every part and place of the universe with which we are acquainted we perceive the exertion of a power which we believe, mediately or immediately, to proceed from the Deity. For instance, in what part or point of space that has ever been explored do we not discover attraction? In what regions do we not find light? In what accessible portion of our globe do we not meet with gravity, magnetism, electricity, together with the properties also and powers of organized substances, of vegetable, or of animated nature? Nay, further, we may ask, what kingdom is there of nature, what corner of space, in which there is anything that can be examined by us, where we do not fall upon contrivance and design? The only reflection perhaps which arises in our minds from this view of the world around us is that the laws of nature everywhere prevail, that they are uniform and universal. But what do you mean by the laws of nature or by any law? Effects are produced by power not by laws. A law cannot execute itself. A law refers us to an agent. Now, an agency so general as that we cannot discover its absence, or assign the place in which some effect of its continued energy is not found, may, in popular language at least, and perhaps without much deviation from philosophical strictness, be called universal; and with not quite the same but with no inconsiderable propriety the person or being in whom that power resides or from whom it is derived may be taken to be omnipresent. He who upholds all things by his power may be said to be everywhere present.

This is called a virtual presence. There is also what metaphysicians denominate an essential ubiquity, and which idea the language of Scripture seems to favor; but the former, I think, goes as far as natural theology carries us.

"Eternity" is a negative idea clothed with a positive name. It supposes, in that to which it is applied, a present existence, and is the negation of a beginning or an end of that existence. As applied to the Deity, it has not been controverted by those who acknowledge a Deity at all. Most assuredly, there never was a time in which nothing existed, because that condition must have continued. The universal *blank* must have remained; nothing could rise up out of it, nothing could ever have existed since, nothing could exist now. In strictness, however, we have no concern with duration prior to that of the visible world. Upon this article, therefore, of theology it is sufficient to know that the contriver necessarily existed before the contrivance.

"Self-existence" is another negative idea, namely, the negation of a preceding cause, as of a progenitor, a maker, an author, a creator.

"Necessary existence" means demonstrable existence.

"Spirituality" expresses an idea made up of a negative part and of a positive part. The negative part consists in the exclusion of some of the known properties of matter, especially of solidity, of the *vis inertiae*, and of gravitation. The positive part comprises perception, thought, will, power, *action;* by which last term is meant the origination of motion, the quality, perhaps, in which resides the essential superiority of spirit over matter, "which cannot move, unless it be moved; and cannot but move, when impelled by another." [8] I apprehend that there can be no difficulty in applying to the Deity both parts of this idea.

[8] Bishop Wilkins' *Principles of Natural Religion*, p. 106. [John Wilkins (1614-72), Bishop of Chester, was a man of liberal views and the author of works in various fields, his most important book being *An Essay Towards a Real Character and a Philosophical Language* (London, 1668). The work here referred to by Paley is *On the Principles and Duties of Natural Religion* (London, 1678), with a preface by John Tillotson (1630-94), Archbishop of Canterbury. In this work aspects of Joseph Butler's *Analogy* (1736) are anticipated.]

CHAPTER TWENTY-FIVE

OF THE UNITY OF THE DEITY

Of the "unity of the Deity," the proof is the *uniformity* of plan observable in the universe. The universe itself is a system, each part either depending upon other parts, or being connected with other parts by some common law of motion, or by the presence of some common substance. One principle of gravitation causes a stone to drop toward the earth and the moon to wheel round it. One law of attraction carries all the different planets about the sun. This philosophers demonstrate. There are also other points of agreement among them, which may be considered as marks of the identity of their origin and of their intelligent Author. In all are found the conveniency and stability derived from gravitation. They all experience vicissitudes of days and nights, and changes of season. They all, at least Jupiter, Mars, and Venus, have the same advantages from their atmosphere as we have. In all the planets, the axes of rotation are permanent. Nothing is more probable than that the same attracting influence, acting according to the same rule, reaches to the fixed stars; but if this be only probable, another thing is certain, namely, that the same element of light does. The light from a fixed star affects our eyes in the same manner, is refracted and reflected according to the same laws, as the light of a candle. The velocity of the light of the fixed stars is also the same as the velocity of the light of the sun, reflected from the satellites of Jupiter. The heat of the sun in kind differs nothing from the heat of a coal fire.

In our own globe the case is clearer. New countries are continually discovered, but the old laws of nature are always found in them; new plants perhaps, or animals, but always in company with plants and animals which we already know, and always possessing many of the same general properties. We never get among such original or totally different modes of existence, as to indicate that we are come into the province of a different Creator or under the direction of a different will. In truth, the same order of things attends us wherever we go. The elements act upon one another, electricity operates, the tides rise and fall, the magnetic needle elects its position in one region of the earth and sea as well as in another. One atmosphere invests all parts of the globe and connects all, one sun illuminates, one moon exerts its specific attraction upon all parts. If there be a variety in natural effects, as, for example, in the tides of different seas, that very variety is the result of the same cause acting under different circumstances. In many cases this is proved; in all, is probable.

The inspection and comparison of *living* forms add to this argument examples without number. Of all large terrestrial animals the structure is very much alike; their senses nearly the same; their natural functions and passions nearly the same; their viscera nearly the same, both in substance, shape, and office; digestion, nutrition, circulation, secretion go on in a similar manner in all; the great circulating fluid is the same, for I think no difference has been discovered in the properties of *blood,* from whatever animal it be drawn. The experiment of transfusion proves that the blood of one animal will serve for another. The *skeletons* also of the larger terrestrial animals show particular varieties, but still under a great general affinity. The resemblance is somewhat less, yet sufficiently evident, between quadrupeds and birds. They are all alike in five respects for one in which they differ.

In *fish,* which belong to another department as it were of nature, the points of comparison become fewer. But we never lose sight of our analogy: for example, we still meet with a stomach, a liver, a spine, with bile and blood, with teeth, with eyes—which eyes are only slightly varied from our own, and which variation, in truth, demonstrates not an interruption but a continuance of the same exquisite plan, for it is the adaptation of the organ to the element, namely, to the different refraction of light passing into the eye out of a denser medium. The provinces, also, themselves of water and earth, are connected by the species of animals which inhabit both, and also by a large tribe of aquatic animals which closely resemble the terrestrial in their internal structure: I mean the cetaceous tribe, which have hot blood, respiring lungs, bowels, and other essential parts like those of land animals. The similitude surely bespeaks the same creation and the same Creator.

Insects and *shellfish* appear to me to differ from other classes of animals the most widely of any. Yet even here, besides many points of particular resemblance, there exists a general relation of a peculiar kind. It is the relation of inversion—the law of contrariety: namely, that whereas, in other animals, the bones, to which the muscles are attached, lie *within* the body, in insects and shellfish they lie on the *outside* of it. The shell of a lobster performs to the animal the office of a *bone,* by furnishing to the tendons that fixed basis or immovable fulcrum without which, mechanically, they could not act. The crust of an insect is its shell and answers the like purpose. The shell also of an oyster stands in the place of a *bone,* the bases of the muscles being fixed to it in the same manner as in other animals they are fixed to the bones. All which, under wonderful varieties indeed, and adaptations of form, confesses an imitation, a remembrance, a carrying on of the same plan.

The observations here made are equally applicable to plants; but, I think, unnecessary to be pursued. It is a very striking circumstance, and also sufficient to prove all which we contend for, that in this part likewise of organized nature we perceive a continuation of the *sexual* system.

Certain however it is that the whole argument for the divine unity goes no further than to a unity of counsel.

It may likewise be acknowledged that no arguments which we are in possession of exclude the ministry of subordinate agents. If such there be, they act under a presiding, a controlling will, because they act according to certain general restrictions, by certain common rules, and, as it should seem, upon a general plan; but still such agents, and different ranks and classes and degrees of them, may be employed.

CHAPTER TWENTY-SIX

OF THE GOODNESS OF THE DEITY

The proof of the *divine goodness* rests upon two propositions, each, as we contend, capable of being made out by observations drawn from the appearances of nature.

The first is "that in a vast plurality of instances in which contrivance is perceived, the design of the contrivance is *beneficial*."

The second, "that the Deity has superadded *pleasure* to animal sensations beyond what was necessary for any other purpose, or when the purpose, so far as it was necessary, might have been effected by the operation of pain."

First, "in a vast plurality of instances in which contrivance is perceived, the design of the contrivance is *beneficial*." No productions of nature display contrivance so manifestly as the parts of animals; and the parts of animals have all of them, I believe, a real, and with very few exceptions, all of them a known and intelligible subserviency to the use of the animal. Now, when the multitude of animals is considered, the number of parts in each, their figure and fitness, the faculties depending upon them, the variety of species, the complexity of structure, the success, in so many cases, and felicity of the result, we can never reflect without the profoundest adoration, upon the character of that Being from whom all these things have proceeded; we cannot help acknowledging what an exertion of benevolence creation was—of a benevolence how minute in its care, how vast in its comprehension!

When we appeal to the parts and faculties of animals, and to the limbs and senses of animals in particular, we state, I conceive, the proper medium of proof for the conclusion which we wish to establish. I will not say that the insensible parts of nature are made solely for the sensitive parts; but this I say, that, when we consider the benevolence of the Deity, we can only consider it in relation to sensitive being. Without this reference, or referred to anything else, the attribute has no object, the term has no meaning. Dead matter is nothing. The parts, therefore, especially the limbs and senses of animals, although they constitute, in mass and quantity, a small portion of the material creation, yet, since they alone are instruments of perception, they compose what may be called the whole of visible nature estimated with a view to the disposition of its author. Consequently, it is in *these* that we are to seek his character. It is by these that we are to prove that the world was made with a benevolent design.

Nor is the design abortive. It is a happy world after all. The air, the earth, the water teem with delighted existence. In a spring moon, or a summer evening, on whichever side I turn my eyes, myriads of happy beings crowd upon my view. "The insect youth are on the wing." Swarms of newborn flies are trying their pinions in the air. Their sportive motions, their wanton mazes, their gratuitous activity, their continual change of place without use or purpose testify their joy and the exultation which they feel in their lately discovered faculties. A bee among the flowers in spring is one of the most cheerful objects that can be looked upon. Its life appears to be all enjoyment, so busy, and so pleased; yet it is only a specimen of insect life with which, by reason of the animal being half domesticated, we happen to be better acquainted than we are with that of others. The whole-winged insect tribe, it is probable, are equally intent upon their proper employments, and, under every variety of constitution, gratified, and perhaps equally gratified, by the offices which the Author of their nature has assigned to them. But the atmosphere is not the only scene of enjoyment for the insect race. Plants are covered with aphids greedily sucking their juices, and constantly, as it should seem, in the act of sucking. It cannot be doubted but that this is a state of gratification. What else should fix them so close to the operation, and so long? Other species are *running about*, with an alacrity in their motions which carries with it every mark of pleasure. Large patches of ground are sometimes half covered with these brisk and sprightly natures. If we look to what the *waters* produce, shoals of the fry of fish frequent the margins of rivers, of lakes, and of the sea itself. These are so happy that they know not what to do with themselves. Their attitudes, their vivacity, their leaps out of the water, their frolics in it, which I have noticed a thousand times with equal attention and amusement, all conduce to show their excess of spirits, and are simply the effects of that excess. Walking by the seaside in a calm evening, upon a sandy shore, and with an ebbing tide, I have frequently remarked the appearance of a dark cloud, or rather a very thick mist, hanging over the edge of the water, to the height perhaps of half a yard, and of the breadth of two or three yards, stretching along the coast as far as the eye could reach, and always retiring with the water. When this cloud came to be examined, it proved to be nothing else than so much space filled with young shrimps in the act of bounding into the air from the shallow margin of the water or from the wet sand. If any motion of a mute animal could express delight, it was this; if they had meant to make signs of their happiness, they could not have done it more intelligibly. Suppose, then, what I have no doubt of, each individual of this number to be in a state of positive enjoyment; what a sum, collectively, of gratification and pleasure have we here before our view!

The young of all animals appear to me to receive pleasure simply from the exercise of their limbs and bodily faculties, without reference to any end to be attained or any use to be answered by the exertion. A child, without knowing anything of the use of language, is in a high degree delighted with being able to speak. Its incessant repetition of a few articulate sounds, or perhaps of the single word which it has learnt to pronounce, proves this point clearly. Nor is it less pleased with its first successful endeavors to walk, or rather to run—which precedes walking—although entirely ignorant of the importance of the attainment to its future life, and even without applying it to any present purpose. A child is delighted with speaking without having anything to say, and with walking without knowing where to go. And prior to both these, I am disposed to believe that the waking hours of infancy are agreeably taken up with the exercise of vision, or perhaps, more properly speaking, with learning to see.

But it is not for youth alone that the great Parent of creation has provided. Happiness is found with the purring cat, no less than with the playful kitten—in the armchair of dozing age, as well as in either the sprightliness of the dance or the animation of the chase. To novelty, to acuteness of sensation, to hope, to ardor of pursuit, succeeds what is, in no inconsiderable degree, an equivalent for them all, "perception of ease." Herein is the exact difference between the young and the old. The young are not happy but when enjoying pleasure; the old are happy when free from pain. And this constitution suits with the degrees of animal power which they respectively possess. The vigor of youth was to be stimulated to action by impatience of rest; while, to the imbecility of age, quietness and repose become positive gratifications. In one important respect, the advantage is with the old. A state of ease is, generally speaking, more attainable than a state of pleasure. A constitution, therefore, which can enjoy ease is preferable to that which can taste only pleasure. This same perception of ease oftentimes renders old age a condition of great comfort, especially when riding at its anchor after a busy or tempestuous life. It is well described by Rousseau [9] to be the interval of repose and enjoyment between the hurry and the end of life. How far the same cause extends to other animal natures cannot be judged of with certainty. The appearance of satisfaction with which most animals, as their activity subsides, seek and enjoy rest affords reason to believe that this source of gratification is appointed to advanced life, under all, or most of its various forms. In the species with which we are best acquainted, namely, our own, I am far, even as an observer of human life, from thinking that youth is its happiest season, much less the only happy one; as a Christian, I am willing

[9] [Jean-Jacques Rousseau (1712-78).]

to believe that there is a great deal of truth in the following representation given by a very pious writer as well as excellent man: "To the intelligent and virtuous, old age presents a scene of tranquil enjoyments, of obedient appetite, of well-regulated affections, of maturity in knowledge, and of calm preparation for immortality. In this serene and dignified state, placed as it were on the confines of two worlds, the mind of a good man reviews what is past with the complacency of an approving conscience; and looks forward with humble confidence in the mercy of God, and with devout aspirations toward his eternal and ever increasing favor." [10]

What is seen in different stages of the same life is still more exemplified in the lives of different animals. Animal enjoyments are infinitely *diversified*. The modes of life to which the organization of different animals respectively determines them are not only of various but of opposite kinds. Yet each is happy in its own. For instance, animals of prey live much alone; animals of milder constitution, in society. Yet the herring which lives in shoals and the sheep which lives in flocks are not more happy in a crowd or more contented among their companions than is the pike or the lion with the deep solitudes of the pool or the forest.

But it will be said that the instances which we have here brought forward, whether of vivacity or repose, or of apparent enjoyment derived from either, are picked and favorable instances. We answer, first, that they are instances, nevertheless, which comprise large provinces of sensitive existence; that every case which we have described is the case of millions. At this moment, in every given moment of time, how many myriads of animals are eating their food, gratifying their appetites, ruminating in their holes, accomplishing their wishes, pursu-

[10] *Father's Instructions* by Dr. Percival of Manchester, p. 317. [Dr. Thomas Percival (1740-1804), English physician and author, friend of David Hume. The book here referred to by Paley was a work, intended for children, which achieved great popularity in the late eighteenth century. It was published originally in 1775, and a concluding part was published in 1800.]

ing their pleasures, taking their pastimes! In each individual, how many things must go right for it to be at ease, yet how large a proportion out of every species is so in every assignable instant. Secondly, we contend, in the terms of our original proposition, that throughout the whole of life, as it is diffused in nature, and as far as we are acquainted with it, looking to the average of sensations, the plurality and the preponderancy is in favor of happiness by a vast excess. In our own species, in which perhaps the assertion may be more questionable than any other, the prepollency of good over evil, of health, for example, and ease, over pain and distress, is evinced by the very notice which calamities excite. What inquiries does the sickness of our friends produce; what conversation, their misfortunes. This shows that the common course of things is in favor of happiness; that happiness is the rule, misery the exception. Were the order reversed, our attention would be called to examples of health and competency instead of disease and want.

One great cause of our insensibility of the goodness of the Creator is the very *extensiveness* of his bounty. We prize but little what we share only in common with the rest or with the generality of our species. When we hear of blessings we think forthwith of successes, of prosperous fortunes, of honors, riches, preferments, that is, of those advantages and superiorities over others which we happen either to possess, or to be in pursuit of, or to covet. The common benefits of our nature entirely escape us. Yet these are the great things. These constitute what most properly ought to be accounted blessings of Providence— what alone, if we might so speak, are worthy of its care. Nightly rest and daily bread, the ordinary use of our limbs and senses and understandings are gifts which admit of no comparison with any other. Yet because almost every man we meet with possesses these, we leave them out of our enumeration. They raise no sentiment, they move no gratitude. Now herein is our judgment perverted by our selfishness. A blessing ought in truth to be the *more* satisfactory, the bounty at least of the donor is rendered more conspicuous, by its very diffusion, its commonness, its cheapness—by its falling to the lot, and forming the happiness of the great bulk and body of our species, as well as of ourselves. Nay, even when we do not possess it, it ought to be matter of thankfulness that others do. But we have a different way of thinking. We court distinction. That is not the worst: we *see* nothing but what has distinction to recommend it. This necessarily contracts our views of the Creator's beneficence within a narrow compass, and most unjustly. It is in those things which are so common as to be [of] no distinction, that the amplitude of the divine benignity is perceived.

But pain, no doubt, and privations exist in numerous instances and to a great degree, which collectively would be very great, if they were compared with any other thing than with the mass of animal fruition. For the application, therefore, of our proposition to that *mixed* state of things which these exceptions induce, two rules are necessary, and both, I think, just and fair rules. One is that we regard those effects alone which are accompanied with proofs of intention; the other, that when we cannot resolve all appearances into benevolence of design, we make the few give place to the many, the little to the great—that we take our judgment from a large and decided preponderancy, if there be one.

I crave leave to transcribe into this place what I have said upon this subject in my *Moral Philosophy:*

> When God created the human species, either he wished their happiness, or he wished their misery, or he was indifferent and unconcerned about either.
>
> If he had wished our misery, he might have made sure of his purpose by forming our senses to be so many sores and pains to us, as they are now instruments of gratification and enjoyment; or by placing us amid objects so ill-suited to our perceptions as to have continually offended us, instead of ministering to our refreshment and delight. He might have made, for example, everything we tasted, bitter; everything we saw, loathsome; everything we touched, a sting; every smell, a stench; and every sound, a discord.
>
> If he had been indifferent about our happiness or misery,

we must impute to our good fortune—as all design by this supposition is excluded—both the capacity of our senses to receive pleasure and the supply of external objects fitted to produce it.

But either of these, and still more both of them, being too much to be attributed to accident, nothing remains but the first supposition that God, when he created the human species, wished their happiness, and made for them the provision which he has made with that view and for that purpose.

The same argument may be proposed in different terms, *thus:* contrivance proves design; and the predominant tendency of the contrivance indicates the disposition of the designer. The world abounds with contrivances; and all the contrivances which we are acquainted with are directed to beneficial purposes. Evil, no doubt, exists but is never, that we can perceive, the *object* of contrivance. Teeth are contrived to eat not to ache; their aching now and then is incidental to the contrivance, perhaps inseparable from it; or even, if you will, let it be called a defect in the contrivance, but it is not the object of it. This is a distinction which well deserves to be attended to. In describing implements of husbandry, you would hardly say of the sickle that it is made to cut the reaper's fingers; though from the construction of the instrument and the manner of using it, this mischief often follows. But if you had occasion to describe instruments of torture or execution, this engine, you would say, is to extend the sinews, this to dislocate the joints, this to break the bones, this to scorch the soles of the feet. Here pain and misery are the very objects of the contrivance. Now nothing of this sort is to be found in the works of nature. We never discover a train of contrivance to bring about an evil purpose. No anatomist ever discovered a system of organization calculated to produce pain and disease, or, in explaining the parts of the human body, ever said, this is to irritate, this to inflame, this duct is to convey the gravel to the kidneys, this gland to secrete the humor which forms the gout; if by chance he come at a part of which he knows not the use, the most he can say is that it is useless; no one ever suspects that it is put there to incommode, to annoy, or to torment.[11]

11 [William Paley, *The Principles of Moral and Political Philosophy* (London, 1785), pp. 63-64.]

The TWO CASES which appear to me to have the most difficulty in them, as forming the most of the appearance of exception to the representation here given, are those of *venomous*
animals and of animals *preying* upon one another. These properties of animals, wherever they are found, must, I think, be
referred to design, because there is in all cases of the first and
in most cases of the second an express and distinct organization provided for the producing of them. Under the first
head, the fangs of vipers, the stings of wasps and scorpions are
as clearly intended for their purpose, as any animal structure
is for any purpose the most incontestably beneficial. And the
same thing must, under the second head, be acknowledged of
the talons and beaks of birds, of the tusks, teeth, and claws of
beasts of prey—of the shark's mouth, of the spider's web, and
of numberless weapons of offense belonging to different tribes
of voracious insects. We cannot, therefore, avoid the difficulty
by saying that the effect was not intended. The only question
open to us is whether it be ultimately evil. From the confessed
and felt imperfection of our knowledge, we ought to presume
that there may be consequences of this economy which are
hidden from us; from the benevolence which pervades the
general designs of nature, we ought also to presume that these
consequences, if they could enter into our calculation, would
turn the balance on the favorable side. Both these I contend to
be reasonable presumptions. Not reasonable presumptions if
these two cases were the only cases which nature presented to
our observation, but reasonable presumptions, under the reflection that the cases in question are combined with a multitude of intentions, all proceeding from the same author, and
all, except these, directed to ends of undisputed utility. Of the
vindications, however, of this economy, which we are able to
assign, such as most extenuate the difficulty, are the following.

With respect to *venomous* bites and stings, it may be observed:

1. That, the animal itself being regarded, the faculty complained of is *good:* being conducive, in all cases, to the defense
of the animal; in some cases, to the subduing of its prey; and

in some, probably, to the killing of it, when caught, by a mortal wound, inflicted in the passage to the stomach, which may be no less merciful to the victim than salutary to the devourer. In the viper, for instance, the poisonous fang may do that which, in other animals of prey, is done by the crush of the teeth. Frogs and mice might be swallowed alive without it.

2. But it will be said that this provision, when it comes to the case of bites, deadly even to human bodies and to those of large quadrupeds, is greatly *overdone;* that it might have fulfilled its use and yet have been much less deleterious than it is. Now I believe the case of bites which produce death in large animals—of stings I think there are none—to be very few. The experiments of the Abbé Fontana,[12] which were numerous, go strongly to the proof of this point. He found that it required the action of five exasperated vipers to kill a dog of a moderate size; but that to the killing of a mouse or a frog, a single bite was sufficient; which agrees with the use which we assign to the faculty. The abbé seemed to be of opinion that the bite even of the rattlesnake would not usually be mortal, allowing, however, that in certain particularly unfortunate cases, as when the puncture had touched some very tender part, pricked a principal nerve, for instance, or, as it is said, some more considerable lymphatic vessel, death might speedily ensue.

3. It has been, I think, very justly remarked concerning serpents that, while only a few species possess the venomous property, that property guards the whole tribe. The most innocuous snake is avoided with as much care as a viper. Now the terror with which large animals regard this class of reptiles is its protection; and this terror is founded on the formidable revenge which a few of the number, compared with the whole, are capable of taking. The species of serpents described by Linnaeus [13] amount to two hundred and eighteen, of which thirty-two only are poisonous.

12 [Felice Fontana (1730-1805), Italian physiologist and naturalist.]
13 [Karl von Linné (1707-78), Swedish naturalist.]

4. It seems to me that animal constitutions are provided not only for each element, but for each state of the elements, that is, for every climate and for every temperature; and that part of the mischief complained of arises from animals—the human animal most especially—occupying situations upon the earth which do not belong to them, nor were ever intended for their habitation. The folly and wickedness of mankind, and necessities proceeding from these causes, have driven multitudes of the species to seek a refuge among burning sands, while countries blessed with hospitable skies and with the most fertile soils remain almost without a human tenant. We invade the territories of wild beasts and venomous reptiles and then complain that we are infested by their bites and stings. Some accounts of Africa place this observation in a strong point of view. "The deserts," says Adamson,[14] "are entirely barren except where they are found to produce serpents, and in such quantities, that some extensive plains are almost entirely covered with them." These are the natures appropriated to the situation. Let them enjoy their existence, let them have their country. Surface enough will be left to man, though his numbers were increased a hundredfold, and left to him where he might live exempt from these annoyances.

The SECOND CASE, namely, that of animals *devouring* one another, furnishes a consideration of much larger extent. To judge whether, as a general provision, this can be deemed an *evil,* even so far as we understand its consequences, which, probably, is a partial understanding, the following reflections are fit to be attended to.

1. Immortality upon this earth is out of the question. Without death there could be no generation, no sexes, no parental relation, that is, as things are constituted, no animal happiness. The particular duration of life assigned to different animals can form no part of the objection; because, whatever that duration be, while it remains finite and limited, it may always be asked why it is no longer. The natural age of different animals varies from a single day to a century of years. No account

14 [Probably a contemporary of Paley, not identifiable.]

can be given of this; nor could any be given, whatever other proportion of life had obtained among them.

The term then of life in different animals being the same as it is, the question is, what mode of taking it away is the best even for the animal itself?

Now, according to the established order of nature—which we must suppose to prevail, or we cannot reason at all upon the subject—the three methods by which life is usually put an end to are acute diseases, decay, and violence. The simple and natural life of *brutes* is not often visited by acute distempers; nor could it be deemed an improvement of their lot if they were. Let it be considered, therefore, in what a condition of suffering and misery a brute animal is placed which is left to perish by *decay*. In human sickness or infirmity there is the assistance of man's rational fellow creatures, if not to alleviate his pains, at least to minister to his necessities and to supply the place of his own activity. A brute, in his wild and natural state, does everything for himself. When his strength, therefore, or his speed, or his limbs, or his senses fail him, he is delivered over either to absolute famine or to the protracted wretchedness of a life slowly wasted by the scarcity of food. Is it then to see the world filled with drooping, superannuated, half-starved, helpless, and unhelped animals, that you would alter the present system of pursuit and prey?

2. Which system is also to them the spring of motion and activity on both sides. The pursuit of its prey forms the employment, and appears to constitute the pleasure of a considerable part of the animal creation. The using of the means of defense, or flight, or precaution forms also the business of another part. And even of this latter tribe we have no reason to suppose that their happiness is much molested by their fears. Their danger exists continually; and in some cases they seem to be so far sensible of it as to provide, in the best manner they can, against it; but it is only when the attack is actually made upon them that they appear to suffer from it. To contemplate the insecurity of their condition with anxiety and dread requires a degree of reflection which, happily for themselves,

they do not possess. A hare, notwithstanding the number of its dangers and its enemies, is as playful an animal as any other.

3. But, to do justice to the question, the system of animal *destruction* ought always to be considered in strict connection with another property of animal care, namely, *superfecundity*. They are countervailing qualities. One subsists by the correction of the other. In treating, therefore, of the subject under this view—which is, I believe, the true one—our business will be, first, to point out the advantages which are gained by the powers in nature of a superabundant multiplication; and then to show that these advantages are so many reasons for appointing that system of animal hostilities which we are endeavoring to account for.

In almost all cases, nature produces her supplies with profusion. A single codfish spawns, in one season, a greater number of eggs than all the inhabitants of England amount to. A thousand other instances of prolific generation might be stated, which, though not equal to this, would carry on the increase of the species with a rapidity which outruns calculation, and to an immeasurable extent. The advantages of such a constitution are two: first, that it tends to keep the world always full; while, secondly, it allows the proportion between the several species of animals to be differently modified, as different purposes require, or as different situations may afford for them room and food. Where this vast fecundity meets with a vacancy fitted to receive the species, there it operates with its whole effect—there it pours in its numbers and replenishes the waste. We complain of what we call the exorbitant multiplication of some troublesome insects, not reflecting that large portions of nature might be left void without it. If the accounts of travelers may be depended upon, immense tracts of forest in North America would be nearly lost to sensitive existence, if it were not for gnats. "In the thinly inhabited regions of America, in which the waters stagnate and the climate is warm, the whole air is filled with crowds of these insects." Thus it is that, where we looked for solitude and deathlike silence, we meet with animation, activity, enjoyment—with a busy, a happy, and a peopled world. Again, hosts of mice are reckoned among the plagues of the northeast part of Europe, whereas vast plains in Siberia, as we learn from good authority, would be lifeless without them. The Caspian deserts are converted by their presence into crowds of warrens. Between the Volga and the Yaik,[15] and in the country of Hyrcania,[16] the ground, says Pallas,[17] is in many places *covered* with little hills raised by the earth cast out in forming the burrows. Do we so envy these blissful abodes as to pronounce the fecundity by which they are supplied with inhabitants to be an evil, a subject of complaint and not of praise? Further, by virtue of this same superfecundity, what we term destruction becomes almost instantly the parent of life. What we call blights are oftentimes legions of animated beings claiming their portion in the bounty of nature. What corrupts the produce of the earth to us prepares it for them. And it is by means of their rapid multiplication that they take possession of their pasture; a slow propagation would not meet the opportunity.

But in conjunction with the occasional use of this fruitfulness, we observe, also, that it allows the proportion between the several species of animals to be differently modified, as different purposes of utility may require. When the forests of America come to be cleared and the swamps drained, our gnats will give place to other inhabitants. If the population of Europe should spread to the north and the east, the mice will retire before the husbandman and the shepherd and yield their station to herds and flocks. In what concerns the human species, it may be a part of the scheme of Providence that the earth should be inhabited by a shifting, or perhaps a circulating population. In this economy it is possible that there may be the following advantages. When old countries are become exceedingly corrupt, similar modes of life, purer morals, and better institutions may rise up in new ones while fresh soils

15 [Rivers in southern Russia.]
16 [The Crimea.]
17 [Peter Simon Pallas (1741-1811), German naturalist and traveler.]

reward the cultivator with more plentiful returns. Thus the different portions of the globe come into use in succession as the residence of man, and, in his absence, entertain other guests, which by their sudden multiplication fill the chasm. In domesticated animals we find the effect of their fecundity to be that we can always command numbers; we can always have as many of any particular species as we please, or as we can support. Nor do we complain of its excess, it being much more easy to regulate abundance than to supply scarcity.

But then this *superfecundity,* though of great occasional use and importance, exceeds the ordinary capacity of nature to receive or support its progeny. All superabundance supposes destruction or must destroy itself. Perhaps there is no species of terrestrial animals whatever which would not overrun the earth, if it were permitted to multiply in perfect safety; or of fish, which would not fill the ocean—at least, if any single species were left to their natural increase without disturbance or restraint, the food of other species would be exhausted by their maintenance. It is necessary, therefore, that the effects of such prolific faculties be curtailed. In conjunction with other checks and limits, all subservient to the same purpose, are the *thinnings* which take place among animals by their action upon one another. In some instances, we ourselves experience, very directly, the use of these hostilities. One species of insect rids us of another species or reduces their ranks. A third species, perhaps, keeps the second within bounds; and birds or lizards are a fence against the inordinate increase by which even these last might infest us. In other, more numerous, and possibly more important instances, this disposition of things, although less necessary or useful to us, and of course less observed by us, may be necessary and useful to certain other species; or even for the preventing of the loss of certain species from the universe—a misfortune which seems to be studiously guarded against. Though there may be the appearance of failure in some of the details of nature's works, in her great purposes there never are. Her species never fail. The provision

which was originally made for continuing the replenishment
of the world has proved itself to be effectual through a long
succession of ages.

What further shows that the system of destruction among
animals holds an express relation to the system of fecundity,
that they are parts indeed of one compensatory scheme, is that
in each species the fecundity bears a proportion to the small-
ness of the animal, to the weakness, to the shortness of its
natural term of life, and to the dangers and enemies by which
it is surrounded. An elephant produces but one calf; a butterfly lays six hundred eggs. Birds of prey seldom produce more
than two eggs; the sparrow tribe and the duck tribe frequently
sit upon a dozen. In the rivers we meet with a thousand min-
nows for one pike; in the sea, a million of herrings for a single
shark. Compensation obtains throughout. Defenselessness and
devastation are repaired by fecundity.

We have dwelt the longer on these considerations because
the subject to which they apply, namely, that of animals *devouring* one another, forms the chief, if not the only instance,
in the works of the Deity, of an economy stamped by marks of
design in which the character of utility can be called in question. The case of *venomous* animals is of much inferior consequence to the case of prey, and, in some degree, is also in-
cluded under it. To both cases it is probable that many more
reasons belong than those of which we are in possession.

Our FIRST PROPOSITION, and that which we have hitherto
been defending,[18] was "that in a vast plurality of instances, in
which contrivance is perceived, the *design* of the contrivance
is *beneficial*."

Our SECOND PROPOSITION is "that the Deity has added *pleasure* to animal sensations beyond what was necessary for any
other purpose, or when the purpose, so far as it was necessary,
might have been effected by the operation of pain."

This proposition may be thus explained. The capacities
which, according to the established course of nature, are *necessary* to the support or preservation of an animal, however

18 [See above, p. 53.]

manifestly they may be the result of an organization contrived for the purpose, can only be deemed an act or a part of the same will as that which decreed the existence of the animal itself; because, whether the creation proceeded from a benevolent or a malevolent being, these capacities must have been given if the animal existed at all. Animal properties, therefore, which fall under this description, do not strictly prove the goodness of God: they may prove the existence of the Deity; they may prove a high degree of power and intelligence: but they do not prove his goodness; forasmuch as they must have been found in any creation which was capable of continuance, although it is possible to suppose that such a creation might have been produced by a being whose views rested upon misery.

But there is a class of properties which may be said to be superadded from an intention expressly directed to happiness —an intention to give a happy existence distinct from the general intention of providing the means of existence; and that is, of capacities for pleasure in cases wherein, so far as the conservation of the individual or of the species is concerned, they were not wanted, or wherein the purpose might have been secured by the operation of pain. The provision which is made of a variety of objects not necessary to life, and ministering only to our pleasures, and the properties given to the necessaries of life themselves, by which they contribute to pleasure as well as preservation, show a further design than that of giving existence.[19]

A single instance will make all this clear. Assuming the

[19] See this topic considered in Dr. Balguy's treatise upon the *Divine Benevolence*. This excellent author first, I think, proposed it, and nearly in the terms in which it is here stated. Some other observations also under this head are taken from that treatise.

[Thomas Balguy (1716-85), English philosopher. The work here referred to by Paley is Balguy's *Divine Benevolence Asserted* (London, 1782), which was part of an unfinished treatise on natural religion. Balguy lectured on moral philosophy and natural theology for a number of years at St. John's College, Cambridge. Paley, it will be recalled, held similar teaching responsibilities at Christ's College, Cambridge, some years later.]

necessity of food for support of animal life, it is requisite that the animal be provided with organs fitted for the procuring, receiving, and digesting of its food. It may also be necessary that the animal be impelled by its sensations to exert its organs. But the pain of hunger would do all this. Why add pleasure to the act of eating; sweetness and relish to food? Why a new and appropriate sense for the perception of the pleasure? Why should the juice of a peach applied to the palate affect the part so differently from what it does when rubbed upon the palm of the hand? This is a constitution which, so far as appears to me, can be resolved into nothing but the pure benevolence of the Creator. Eating is necessary, but the pleasure attending it is not necessary; and that this pleasure depends not only upon our being in possession of the sense of taste, which is different from every other, but upon a particular state of the organ in which it resides, a felicitous adaptation of the organ to the object, will be confessed by anyone who may happen to have experienced that vitiation of taste which frequently occurs in fevers, when every taste is irregular and every one bad.

In mentioning the gratifications of the palate, it may be said that we have made choice of a trifling example. I am not of that opinion. They afford a share of enjoyment to man; but to brutes I believe that they are of very great importance. A horse at liberty passes a great part of his waking hours in eating. To the ox, the sheep, the deer, and other ruminating animals, the pleasure is doubled. Their whole time almost is divided between browsing upon their pasture and chewing their cud. Whatever the pleasure be, it is spread over a large portion of their existence. If there be animals, such as the lupous [20] fish, which swallow their prey whole and at once, without any time, as it should seem, for either drawing out or relishing the taste in the mouth, is it an improbable conjecture that the seat of taste with them is in the stomach, or at least that a sense of pleasure, whether it be taste or not, accompanies the dissolution of the food in that receptacle,

20 [Wolflike, i.e., voracious.]

which dissolution in general is carried on very slowly? If this opinion be right, they are more than repaid for the defect of palate. The feast lasts as long as the digestion.

In seeking for argument we need not stay to insist upon the comparative importance of our example; for the observation holds equally of all, or of three at least of the other senses. The necessary purposes of hearing might have been answered without harmony; of smell, without fragrance; of vision, without beauty. Now "if the Deity had been indifferent about our happiness or misery, we must impute to our good fortune—as all design by this supposition is excluded—both the capacity of our senses to receive pleasure and the supply of external objects fitted to excite it." I allege these as *two* felicities, for they are different things, yet both necessary: the sense being formed, the objects which were applied to it might not have suited it; the objects being fixed, the sense might not have agreed with them. A coincidence is here required which no accident can account for. There are three possible suppositions upon the subject and no more. The first, that the sense, by its original constitution, was made to suit the object; the second, that the object, by its original constitution, was made to suit the sense; the third, that the sense is so constituted as to be able, either universally or within certain limits, by habit and familiarity, to render every object pleasant. Whichever of these suppositions we adopt, the effect evinces on the part of the Author of nature a studious benevolence. If the pleasures which we derive from any of our senses depend upon an original congruity between the sense and the properties perceived by it, we know by experience that the adjustment demanded, with respect to the qualities which were conferred upon the objects that surround us, not only choice and selection, out of a boundless variety of possible qualities with which these objects might have been endued, but a *proportioning also of degree,* because an excess of defect of intensity spoils the perception as much almost as an error in the kind and nature of the quality. Likewise the degree of dullness or acuteness in the sense itself is no arbitrary thing, but, in order to preserve the congruity here spoken of, requires to be in an exact or near correspondency with the strength of the impression. The dullness of the senses forms the complaint of old age. Persons in fevers, and I believe in most maniacal cases, experience great torment from their preternatural acuteness. An increased no less than an impaired sensibility induces a state of disease and suffering.

The doctrine of a specific congruity between animal senses and their objects is strongly favored by what is observed of insects in the election of their food. Some of these will feed upon one kind of plant or animal and upon no other; some caterpillars upon the cabbage alone, some upon the black currant alone. The species of caterpillar which eats the vine will starve upon the alder; nor will that which we find upon fennel touch the rosebush. Some insects confine themselves to two or three kinds of plants or animals. Some, again, show so strong a preference, as to afford reason to believe that, though they may be driven by hunger to others, they are led by the pleasure of taste to a few particular plants alone; and all this, as it should seem, independently of habit or imitation.

But should we accept the third hypothesis and even carry it so far as to ascribe everything which concerns the question to habit—as in certain species, the human species most particularly, there is reason to attribute something—we have then before us an animal capacity, not less perhaps to be admired than the native congruities which the other scheme adopts. It cannot be shown to result from any fixed necessity in nature that what is frequently applied to the senses should of course become agreeable to them. It is, so far as it subsists, a power of accommodation provided in these senses by the Author of their structure, and forms a part of their perfection.

In whichever way we regard the senses, they appear to be specific gifts, ministering not only to preservation but to pleasure. But what we usually call the *senses* are probably themselves far from being the only vehicles of enjoyment, or the whole of our constitution which is calculated for the same purpose. We have many internal sensations of the most agreeable kind, hardly referable to any of the five senses. Some physiologists have held that all secretion is pleasurable; and that the complacency which in health, without any external assignable object to excite it, we derive from life itself is the effect of our secretions going on well within us. All this may be true; but if true, what reason can be assigned for it, except the will of the Creator? It may reasonably be asked, why is anything a pleasure? And I know no answer which can be returned to the question but that which refers it to appointment.

We can give no account whatever of our pleasures in the simple and original perception; and even when physical sensations are assumed, we can seldom account for them in the secondary and complicated shapes in which they take the name of diversions. I never yet met with a sportsman who could tell me in what the sport consisted—who could resolve it into its principle and state that principle. I have been a great follower of fishing myself and in its cheerful solitude have passed some of the happiest hours of a sufficiently happy life; but to this moment I could never trace out the source of the pleasure which it afforded me.

The "quantum in rebus inane!" [21] whether applied to our amusements or to our graver pursuits, to which, in truth, it sometimes equally belongs, is always an unjust complaint. If trifles engage, and if trifles make us happy, the true reflection suggested by the experiment is upon the tendency of nature to gratification and enjoyment; which is, in other words, the goodness of its Author toward his sensitive creation.

Rational natures also, as such, exhibit qualities which help to confirm the truth of our position. The degree of understanding found in mankind is usually much greater than what is necessary for mere preservation. The pleasure of choosing for themselves and of prosecuting the object of their choice should seem to be an original source of enjoyment. The pleasures received from things great, beautiful, or new, from imitation or from the liberal arts, are in some measure not only

[21] ["How much triviality there is in things!"]

superadded but unmixed gratifications, having no pains to balance them.[22]

I do not know whether our attachment to *property* be not something more than the mere dictate of reason, or even than the mere effect of association. Property communicates a charm to whatever is the object of it. It is the first of our abstract ideas; it cleaves to us the closest and the longest. It endears to the child its plaything, to the peasant his cottage, to the landholder his estate. It supplies the place of prospect and scenery. Instead of coveting the beauty of distant situations, it teaches every man to find it in his own. It gives boldness and grandeur to plains and fens, tinge and coloring to clays and fallows.

All these considerations come in aid of our *second* proposition. The reader will now bear in mind what our two propositions were. They were, firstly, that in a vast plurality of instances in which contrivance is perceived, the design of the contrivance is beneficial; secondly, that the Deity has added pleasure to animal sensations beyond what was necessary for any other purpose, or when the purpose, so far as it was necessary, might have been effected by the operation of pain.

While these propositions can be maintained, we are authorized to ascribe to the Deity the character of benevolence; and what is benevolence at all must in him be *infinite* benevolence, by reason of the infinite, that is to say, the incalculably great number of objects upon which it is exercised.

Of the ORIGIN OF EVIL, no universal solution has been discovered; I mean, no solution which reaches to all cases of complaint. The most comprehensive is that which arises from the consideration of *general rules*. We may, I think, without much difficulty, be brought to admit the four following points: first, that important advantages may accrue to the universe from the order of nature proceeding according to general laws; secondly, that general laws, however well set and constituted, often thwart and cross one another; thirdly, that from these thwartings and crossings frequent particular inconveniences

22 Balguy on the *Divine Benevolence*. [See above, note 19, p. 69.]

will arise; and fourthly, that it agrees with our observations to suppose that some degree of these inconveniences takes place in the works of nature. These points may be allowed; and it may also be asserted that the general laws with which we are acquainted are directed to beneficial ends. On the other hand, with many of these laws we are not acquainted at all, or we are totally unable to trace them in their branches and in their operation; the effect of which ignorance is that they cannot be of importance to us as measures by which to regulate our conduct. The conservation of them may be of importance in other respects, or to other beings, but we are uninformed of their value or use; uninformed, consequently, when and how far they may or may not be suspended, or their effects turned aside by a presiding and benevolent will, without incurring greater evils than those which would be avoided. The consideration, therefore, of general laws, although it may concern the question of the origin of evil very nearly, which I think it does, rests in views disproportionate to our faculties, and in a knowledge which we do not possess. It serves rather to account for the obscurity of the subject than to supply us with distinct answers to our difficulties. However, while we assent to the above-stated propositions as principles, whatever uncertainty we may find in the application, we lay a ground for believing that cases of apparent evil, for which *we* can suggest no particular reason, are governed by reasons which are more general, which lie deeper in the order of second causes, and which on that account are removed to a greater distance from us.

The doctrine of *imperfections,* or, as it is called, of evils of imperfection, furnishes an account, founded, like the former, in views of universal nature. The doctrine is briefly this: it is probable that creation may be better replenished by sensitive beings of different sorts than by sensitive beings all of one sort. It is likewise probable that it may be better replenished by different orders of beings rising one above another in gradation than by beings possessed of equal degrees of perfection. Now, a gradation of such beings implies a gradation of imperfections. No class can justly complain of the imperfections which belong to its place in the scale, unless it were allowable for it to complain that a scale of being was appointed in nature; for which appointment there appear to be reasons of wisdom and goodness.

In like manner, *finiteness,* or what is resolvable into finiteness, in inanimate subjects, can never be a just subject of complaint; because if it were ever so, it would be always so: we mean that we can never reasonably demand that things should be larger or more, when the same demand might be made whatever the quantity or number was.

And to me it seems that the sense of mankind has so far acquiesced in these reasons, as that we seldom complain of evils of this class when we clearly perceive them to be such. What I have to add, therefore, is that we ought not to complain of some other evils which stand upon the same foot of vindication as evils of confessed imperfection. We never complain that the globe of our earth is too small, nor should we complain if it were even much smaller. But where is the difference to us, between a less globe and part of the present being uninhabitable? The inhabitants of an island may be apt enough to murmur at the sterility of some parts of it, against its rocks, or sands, or swamps; but no one thinks himself authorized to murmur simply because the island is not larger than it is. Yet these are the same griefs.

The above are the two metaphysical answers which have been given to this great question. They are not the worse for being metaphysical, provided they be founded—which I think they are—in right reasoning; but they are of a nature too wide to be brought under our survey, and it is often difficult to apply them in the detail. Our speculations, therefore, are perhaps better employed when they confine themselves within a narrower circle.

The observations which follow are of this more limited, but more determinate kind.

Of *bodily pain,* the principal observation, no doubt, is that which we have already made and already dwelt upon, namely, "that it is seldom the object of contrivance; that when it is so, the contrivance rests ultimately in good."

To which, however, may be added that the annexing of pain to the means of destruction is a salutary provision, inasmuch as it teaches vigilance and caution: [it] both gives notice of danger, and excites those endeavors which may be necessary to preservation. The evil consequence which sometimes arises from the want of that timely intimation of danger which pain gives is known to the inhabitants of cold countries by the example of frostbitten limbs. I have conversed with patients who had lost toes and fingers by this cause. They have in general told me that they were totally unconscious of any local uneasiness at the time. Some I have heard declare that, while they were about their employment, neither their situation nor the state of the air was unpleasant. They felt no pain, they suspected no mischief, till, by the application of warmth, they discovered, too late, the fatal injury which some of their extremities had suffered. I say that this shows the use of pain, and that we stand in need of such a monitor. I believe also that the use extends farther than we suppose or can now trace; that to disagreeable sensations we and all animals owe, or have owed, many habits of action which are salutary, but which are become so familiar as not easily to be referred to their origin.

PAIN also itself is not without its *alleviations*. It may be violent and frequent, but it is seldom both violent and long continued; and its pauses and intermissions become positive pleasures. It has the power of shedding a satisfaction over intervals of ease, which I believe few enjoyments exceed. A man resting from a fit of the stone or gout is, for the time, in possession of feelings which undisturbed health cannot impart. They may be dearly bought, but still they are to be set against the price. And indeed it depends upon the duration and urgency of the pain, whether they be dearly bought or not. I am far from being sure that a man is not a gainer by suffering a moderate interruption of bodily ease for a couple of hours out of the four and twenty. Two very common observations favor this opinion: one is that remissions of pain call forth from those who experience them stronger expressions of satisfaction and of gratitude toward both the author and the instruments of their relief, than are excited by advantages of any other kind; the second is that the spirits of sick men do not sink in proportion to the acuteness of their sufferings, but rather appear to be roused and supported, not by pain, but by the high degree of comfort which they derive from its cessation, or even its subsidency, whenever that occurs; and which they taste with a relish that diffuses some portion of mental complacency over the whole of that mixed state of sensations in which disease has placed them.

In connection with bodily pain may be considered bodily *disease*, whether painful or not. Few diseases are fatal. I have before me the account of a dispensary in the neighborhood, which states six years' experience as follows:

Admitted	6,420
Cured	5,476
Dead	234

And this I suppose nearly to agree with what other similar institutions exhibit. Now, in all these cases, some disorder must have been felt, or the patients would not have applied for a remedy; yet we see how large a proportion of the maladies which were brought forward have either yielded to proper treatment or, what is more probable, ceased of their own accord. We owe these frequent recoveries, and, where recovery does not take place, this patience of the human constitution under many of the distempers by which it is visited, to two benefactions of our nature. One is that she works within certain limits, allows of a certain latitude within which health may be preserved, and within the confines of which it only suffers a graduated diminution. Different quantities of food, different degrees of exercise, different portions of sleep, different states of the atmosphere are compatible with the possession of health. So likewise it is with the secretions and excretions, with many internal functions of the body, and with

the state, probably, of most of its internal organs. They may
vary considerably not only without destroying life but without
occasioning any high degree of inconveniency. The other
property of our nature, to which we are still more beholden,
is its constant endeavor to restore itself, when disordered, to
its regular course. The fluids of the body appear to possess a
power of separating and expelling any noxious substance
which may have mixed itself with them. This they do, in erup-
tive fevers, by a kind of despumation, as Sydenham [23] calls it,
analogous in some measure to the intestine action by which
fermenting liquors work the yeast to the surface. The solids,
on their part, when their action is obstructed, not only resume
that action as soon as the obstruction is removed, but they
struggle with the impediment. They take an action as near to
the true one as the difficulty and the disorganization with
which they have to contend will allow of.

Of *mortal* diseases, the great use is to reconcile us to death.
The horror of death proves the value of life. But it is in the
power of disease to abate or even extinguish this horror, which
it does in a wonderful manner and oftentimes by a mild and
imperceptible gradation. Every man who has been placed in
a situation to observe it is surprised with the change which
has been wrought in himself, when he compares the view
which he entertains of death upon a sickbed, with the heart-
sinking dismay with which he should some time ago have met
it in health. There is no similitude between the sensations of
a man led to execution and the calm expiring of a patient at
the close of his disease. Death to him is only the last of a long
train of changes, in his progress through which it is possible
that he may experience no shocks or sudden transitions.

Death itself, as a mode of removal and of succession, is so
connected with the whole order of our animal world that almost everything in that world must be changed to be able to
do without it. It may seem likewise impossible to separate the
fear of death from the enjoyment of life, or the perception of
that fear from rational natures. Brutes are in a great measure

23 [Thomas Sydenham (1624-89), English physician.]

delivered from all anxiety on this account by the inferiority of their faculties; or rather, they seem to be armed with the apprehension of death just sufficiently to put them upon the means of preservation, and no further. But would a human being wish to purchase this immunity at the expense of those mental powers which enable him to look forward to the future?

Death implies *separation;* and the loss of those whom we love must necessarily, so far as we can conceive, be accompanied with pain. To the brute creation, nature seems to have stepped in with some secret provision for their relief under the rupture of their attachments. In their instincts toward their offspring, and of their offspring to them, I have often been surprised to observe how ardently they love and how soon they forget. The pertinacity of human sorrow—upon which time also at length lays its softening hand—is probably, therefore, in some manner connected with the qualities of our rational or moral nature. One thing, however, is clear, namely, that it is better that we should possess affections, the sources of so many virtues and so many joys, although they be exposed to the incidents of life as well as the interruptions of mortality, than, by the want of them, be reduced to a state of selfishness, apathy, and quietism.

Of other external evils—still confining ourselves to what are called physical or natural evils—a considerable part come within the scope of the following observation: the great principle of human satisfaction is *engagement.* It is a most just distinction, which the late Mr. Tucker [24] has dwelt upon so largely in his works, between pleasures in which we are passive and pleasures in which we are active. And I believe every attentive observer of human life will assent to his position, that however grateful the sensations may occasionally be in which we are passive, it is not these but the latter class of our pleas-

24 [Abraham Tucker (1705-74), English philosopher, humorist, author of *The Light of Nature Pursued,* the first four volumes of which were published in 1768 and the last three posthumously published in 1778. Paley expresses his deep indebtedness to Tucker in the preface of his own work, *The Principles of Moral and Political Philosophy* (London, 1785).]

ures which constitute satisfaction—which supply that regular stream of moderate and miscellaneous enjoyments in which happiness, as distinguished from voluptuousness, consists. Now for rational occupation, which is, in other words, the very material of contented existence, there would be no place left, if either the things with which we had to do were absolutely impracticable to our endeavors, or if they were too obedient to our uses. A world furnished with advantages on one side, and beset with difficulties, wants, and inconveniences on the other, is the proper abode of free, rational, and active natures, being the fittest to stimulate and exercise their faculties. The very *refractoriness* of the objects they have to deal with contributes to this purpose. A world in which nothing depended upon ourselves, however it might have suited an imaginary race of beings, would not have suited mankind. Their skill, prudence, industry—their various arts and their best attainments, from the application of which they draw, if not their highest, their most permanent gratifications, would be insignificant, if things could be either molded by our volitions, or, of their own accord, conformed themselves to our views and wishes. Now it is in this refractoriness that we discern the seed and principle of *physical* evil, as far as it arises from that which is external to us.

.   .   .   .

CHAPTER TWENTY-SEVEN

CONCLUSION

In all cases wherein the mind feels itself in danger of being confounded by variety, it is sure to rest upon a few strong points, or perhaps upon a single instance. Among a multitude of proofs it is *one* that does the business. If we observe in any argument that hardly two minds fix upon the same instance, the diversity of choice shows the strength of the argument because it shows the number and competition of the examples. There is no subject in which the tendency to dwell upon select or single topics is so usual because there is no subject of which, in its full extent, the latitude is so great as that of natural history applied to the proof of an intelligent Creator. For my part, I take my stand in human anatomy; and the examples of mechanism I should be apt to draw out from the copious catalogue which it supplies are the pivot upon which the head turns, the ligaments within the socket of the hip-joint, the pulley or trochlear muscles of the eye, the epiglottis, the bandages which tie down the tendons of the wrist and instep, the slit or perforated muscles at the hands and feet, the knitting of the intestines to the mesentery, the course of the chyle into the blood, and the constitution of the sexes as extended throughout the whole of the animal creation. To these instances the reader's memory will go back, as they are severally set forth in their places: there is not one of the number which I do not think decisive—not one which is not strictly mechanical; nor have I read or heard of any solution of these appearances, which in the smallest degree shakes the conclusion that we build upon them.

But of the greatest part of those who, either in this book or any other, read arguments to prove the existence of a God, it will be said that they leave off only where they began; that they were never ignorant of this great truth, never doubted of it; that it does not therefore appear what is gained by researches from which no new opinion is learned, and upon the subject of which no proofs were wanted. Now, I answer that by *investigation* the following points are always gained in favor of doctrines even the most generally acknowledged, supposing them to be true, namely, stability and impression. Occasions will arise to try the firmness of our most habitual opinions. And upon these occasions it is a matter of incalculable use to feel our foundation, to find a support in argument for what we had taken up upon authority. In the present case the arguments upon which the conclusion rests are exactly such as a truth of universal concern ought to rest upon. "They are sufficiently open to the views and capacities of the unlearned, at the same time that they acquire new strength and luster from the discoveries of the learned." If they had been altogether abstruse and recondite, they would not have found their way to the understandings of the mass of mankind; if they had been merely popular, they might have wanted solidity.

But, secondly, what is gained by research in the stability of our conclusion is also gained from it in *impression*. Physicians tell us that there is a great deal of difference between taking a medicine and the medicine getting into the constitution; a difference not unlike which, obtains with respect to those great moral propositions which ought to form the directing principles of human conduct. It is one thing to assent to a proposition of this sort; another, and a very different thing, to have properly imbibed its influence. I take the case to be this: perhaps almost every man living has a particular train of thought, into which his mind glides and falls, when at leisure from the impressions and ideas that occasionally excite it; perhaps, also, the train of thought here spoken of, more than any other thing, determines the character. It is of the utmost consequence, therefore, that this property of our constitution be well regulated. Now it is by frequent or continued meditation upon a subject, by placing a subject in different points of view, by induction of particulars, by variety of examples, by applying principles to the solution of phenomena, by dwelling upon proofs and consequences, that mental exercise is drawn into any particular channel. It is by these means, at least, that we have any power over it. The train of spontaneous thought, and the choice of that train, may be directed to different ends, and may appear to be more or less judiciously fixed, according to the purpose in respect of which we consider it; but, in a *moral view,* I shall not, I believe, be contradicted when I say that, if one train of thinking be more desirable than another, it is that which regards the phenomena of nature with a constant reference to a supreme intelligent Author. To have made this the ruling, the habitual sentiment of our minds, is to have laid the foundation of everything which is religious. The world thenceforth becomes a temple, and life itself one continued act of adoration. The change is no less than this: that whereas formerly God was seldom in our thoughts, we can now scarcely look upon anything without perceiving its relation to him. Every organized natural body, in the provisions which it contains for its sustentation and propagation, testifies a care, on the part of the Creator, expressly directed to these purposes. We are on all sides surrounded by such bodies: examined in their parts, wonderfully diversified. So that the mind, as well as the eye, may either expatiate in variety and multitude or fix itself down to the investigation of particular divisions of the science. And in either case it will rise up from its occupation, possessed by the subject in a very different manner, and with a very different degree of influence, from what a mere assent to any verbal proposition which can be formed concerning the existence of the Deity—at least that merely complying assent with which those about us are satisfied, and with which we are too apt to satisfy ourselves—will or can produce upon the thoughts. More especially may this difference be perceived in the degree of admiration and of awe with which the Divinity is regarded, when represented to the understanding by its own remarks, its own reflections, and its own reasonings, compared with what is excited by any language that can be used by others. The works of nature want only to be contemplated. When contemplated, they have everything in them which can astonish by their greatness; for, of the vast scale of operation through which our discoveries carry us, at one end we see an intelligent Power arranging planetary systems, fixing, for instance, the trajectory of *Saturn,* or constructing a ring of two hundred thousand miles diameter, to surround his body, and be suspended like a magnificent arch over the heads of his inhabitants; and, at the other, bending a hooked tooth, concerting and providing an appropriate mechanism for the clasping and reclasping of the filaments of the feather of the hummingbird. We have proof not only of both these works proceeding from an intelligent agent but of their proceeding from the same agent: for, in the first place, we can trace an identity of the plan, a connection of system, from Saturn to our own globe; and when arrived upon our globe, we can, in the second place, pursue the connection through all the organized, especially the animated bodies which it supports. We can observe marks of a common relation, as well to one another as to the elements of which their habitation is composed. Therefore, one mind has planned or at least has prescribed a general plan for all these productions. One Being has been concerned in all.

Under this stupendous Being we live. Our happiness, our existence, is in his hand. All we expect must come from him. Nor ought we to feel our situation insecure. In every nature, and in every portion of nature which we can descry, we find attention bestowed upon even the minutest parts. The hinges in the wings of an earwig, and the joints of its antennae, are as highly wrought as if the Creator had had nothing else to finish. We see no signs of diminution of care by multiplicity of objects, or of distraction of thought by variety. We have no reason to fear, therefore, our being forgotten, or overlooked, or neglected.

The existence and character of the Deity is, in every view, the most interesting of all human speculations. In none, however, is it more so than as it facilitates the belief of the fundamental articles of *revelation*. It is a step to have it proved that there must be something in the world more than what we see. It is a further step to know, that among the invisible things of nature there must be an intelligent mind concerned in its production, order, and support. These points being assured to us by natural theology, we may well leave to revelation the disclosure of many particulars which our research cannot reach respecting either the nature of this Being as the original cause of all things, or his character and designs as a moral governor; and not only so, but the more full confirmation of other particulars, of which, though they do not lie altogether beyond our reasonings and our probabilities, the certainty is by no means equal to the importance. The true theist will be the first to listen to *any* credible communication of divine knowledge. Nothing which he has learnt from natural theology will diminish his desire of further instruction, or his disposition to receive it with humility and thankfulness. He wishes for light, he rejoices in light. His inward veneration of this great Being will incline him to attend with the utmost seriousness, not only to all that can be discovered concerning him by researches into nature, but to all that is taught by a revelation which gives reasonable proof of having proceeded from him.

. . . .

INDEX

The Library of Liberal Arts

The American Heritage Series

· ·